YOUR
EVERYTHING
IS
HIS ANYTHING

YOUR
EVERYTHING
IS
HIS
ANYTHING

Expand Your View of What Prayer and Faith Can Do

JESSE DUPLANTIS

Published by Harrison House Publishers
Shippensburg, PA 17257

ISBN 13 TP: 9781680314496
ISBN 13 eBook: 9781680314502
ISBN 13 HC: 9781680314571
ISBN 13 LP: 9781680314564

For Worldwide Distribution, Printed in the U.S.A.

2 3 4 5 6 7 8 / 23 22 21 20 19

Contents

Introduction: Your *"Everything"* Is His *"Anything"* 7

Chapter 1: What Does *"Whatsoever"* Mean to You? 11

Chapter 2: What Does It Mean to Live a "Shall Not *Want"* Life? . . . 29

Chapter 3: Do You Realize the Power of Jesus' *Name?* 47

Chapter 4: Why *Not* Give God Glory? 63

Chapter 5: What About Asking *"Amiss"*—What About
Asking for What's Not Right in God's Sight? 77

Chapter 6: Why *Not* Let Go and Grow? 87

Chapter 7: Why *Not* Give God What He Wishes? 111

Chapter 8: Why *Not* Give God Pleasure? 133

Chapter 9: Why Would Anyone Deliberately *Limit* God? 167

Chapter 10: Will You Give God *Honor?* 175

Chapter 11: When Will We Believe What Jesus Says
About What *We* Say? 195

Prayer of Salvation 211

About the Author 215

Your "Everything" Is His "Anything"

Expand Your View of What Prayer and Faith Can Do

What I'm going to share with you now began as I was praying one day and seeking God for what He wanted me to preach and share in letters to my partners and friends. Every time I prepare messages, I pray about what God would have me say. I don't want it to be my idea; I want His will. Well, that day, in the middle of my praying, I heard the Lord speak this to my heart:

"Your <u>everything</u> is My <u>anything</u>."

I had no idea what it meant, and so I asked Him, "What does that mean, Lord?" And He immediately led me to open my Bible to a passage that *nobody* believes. That's right! Even though Jesus said it, nobody believes it! It's too controversial. And yet *this* is what the Lord urged me to not only read and meditate on, but to believe…and to share with you, too.

*And **whatsoever** ye shall **ask** in **My name**, **that will I do**, that the Father may be **glorified** in the Son. If ye shall ask **any thing** in My name, I will do it.*

John 14:13-14

It's definitely one of the most controversial things Jesus ever said, but this is what God keeps having me talk about nearly everywhere I go. It's important, and Jesus wouldn't have said it if it wasn't.

Now, you might be thinking the same thing I thought when I read John 14:13-14 and didn't just gloss over it—that it's *hard* to believe it's true. But remember, these are the words of Jesus Christ. *Jesus.* I like to joke that you've got to believe it because…it's in red!

It's time to expand our view of what God can do. Because no matter what anybody in church or out of church says, we *can* receive not only what we *need* but what we *want* from God— and according to Jesus Himself, although the Church world might disagree, neither He nor the Father God in Heaven mind at all! In fact, Jesus said that it brings glory to God when you get "whatsoever" you want. Think about that.

Oh, the controversy of believing God's Word! But, hey, controversy isn't the enemy—the devil is. So, forget about what "they" think and say about what *you* should have in life. What do they know about what God has put on *your* heart? I'll tell you: They don't know anything about God's will for your life. They're not supposed to because they aren't living your life; you are! And I believe the Word shows us that God wants you to live life with more joy, more peace, and yes, more blessings— spiritually, physically, financially, or in any other area that you desire.

Thanks in advance for taking this journey with me. I believe it's time to expand your view of what God can do. I pray that even before you finish this book, you'll be inspired to have the courage it takes to dive into your own heart and see what good desires you have stirring inside.

I pray that you'll have a greater understanding of God's love and goodwill toward you—that you'll give yourself scriptural permission to not only "ask" the Lord for what's on your heart, but to actually *believe* that you can receive what's on your heart. Because you can! It's my prayer that "whatsoever" God has put on your heart will come to pass in your life.

CHAPTER ONE

What Does "Whatsoever" Mean to You?

"And whatsoever ye shall ask in My name, that will I do, that the Father may be glorified in the Son. If ye shall ask any thing in My name, I will do it."

John 14:13-14

What does "whatsoever" mean to you? What do you think "whatsoever" meant to Christ? I'll tell you: "Whatsoever" means and includes *everything*. Yes, you read that right. *Everything*.

What does "ask *anything* in My name" mean to you? I think it means the same to me as everybody else. Anything means anything! Now, whether we believe it or not, Jesus said it. As I meditated on those verses, I began to wonder why I spent so much time talking to God about needs if He'd already agreed to supply them. I started to wonder why so many believers who know Jesus died for them, gave His life for them, and redeemed them seemed to feel so stinking guilty for asking God for anything *more* than needs.

Is "Whatsoever" Only About Needs?

Needs. At one time, needs were all I felt really comfortable praying about when it came to myself or my ministry. I had no problem bringing my requests to God in prayer, just as long as it was something I knew that I really *needed.*

God always met my needs—and the only problem with that was that, well, in my own mind, I seemed to live from one need to the next. Many people live like this. I'd say most Christians I meet think this way, too. But John 14:13-14 changed the way I viewed asking God for anything at all.

It was hard at first for me to wrap my head around those verses because it is so unbelievable to think that all we have to do is *ask*—but God wouldn't let me gloss over His Son's words. Over and over, He kept bringing these verses up to me. And it wasn't long before I realized that just like many other believers, I'd been thinking so far below what Jesus Christ wanted.

Philippians 4:19 said God would supply all our *needs* according to His riches in glory—I knew that verse so well. And yet here were Jesus' words in John 14:13-14, and they went far beyond mere needs. I started to ask myself what "whatsoever" meant to me. In fact, I started asking a lot of questions, and exploring what life might be like if we all took Jesus at His Word…if we didn't just focus on asking for what we *need* in life, but instead started thinking bigger.

We say we believe that God is good. We say we believe everything Jesus said is true. Why then do so many people pray in guilt, as if they are putting God out by asking for anything but needs? Why is there guilt surrounding wants or desires of the heart?

Over and over, God has been bringing John 14:13-14 up to me and nudging me to go deeper when it comes to my "asking anything" in prayer. I don't believe He wants us to shrink back in guilt—that only hinders us from being honest in our prayers and speaking with confidence to the Father about what we really *want*. It's not like He doesn't already know what we want. But He requires that we speak up and have faith in Him—we can't hold on to doubt about God's very nature. God is love and He is a good Father. Jesus only said what the Father told Him to say, and only did what the Father told Him to do.

Now, I believe in the power of faith. In my life and ministry, I've found out that it takes faith to receive anything from God—and I know that praying from a starting place of doubt is like shooting yourself in the foot before you try to run a race.

Doubt and disappointment always go hand in hand. After all, how *can* you expect to receive anything from God if you don't believe He *will* do what He said in the first place? And how successful in receiving will you be if you ask for something you think you *shouldn't* want at all? Our heart and mind must be on the same page.

Is "Everything" Included in "Ask Anything"?

I was raised like a lot of people—with a lot of negativity. I was constantly told what I couldn't have and couldn't do. When I was a kid and people asked what religion my family was, I made a joke: "Pick one! We've been there." I was born, christened, and confirmed a Catholic after my mom and daddy went searching for a church.

My dad had been healed of blindness in his own bedroom after an accident in the oil field took his sight. Being a working man with no other skills that he knew of, he locked the door to the bedroom and started crying and calling out to a God he didn't even know. My mother was banging on the door, but he didn't listen to her. He was intent on reaching God, not just because he couldn't see but because he couldn't "see" any other way to live and feed his family than to be able to work a decent job. At some point in his loud praying, he said something like, "God, if You heal me, I promise I'll raise my kids to know You." Well, God showed up and showed out. My dad fell asleep crying and woke up seeing—and that started us on a church-finding journey that lasted my whole childhood.

So, I've been to a lot of churches. I've heard a lot of truth and a lot of lies about God. I wondered why everybody who said they believed in healing was always sick. I wondered why everybody who said God would take care of them was always broke. It wasn't until I grew up, left the God stuff behind entirely, went into the rock music business, and made a lot of money that I realized that half of the junk I was doing was just to get away from the lies of my childhood in church.

You see, God is good—but when you constantly hear that He isn't, why would any kid on the planet want to follow Him? If you're told that God will beat you, bust you up, hurt you, and throw lightning bolts at you if you do wrong—but if you "endure to the end," you'll be saved—why would anybody want to get saved early?! "Just wait to the end," is what I used to say as a kid.

Later in life, I found out that God wasn't even like that after I watched Billy Graham on television—something I didn't even want to do, but my wife made a snide comment, and so I sat down and watched. God reached out to me as I sat on that bed, all dressed to go play rock music. My plan had been to go play, go get drunk, do some drugs, and run around with some women. God had other plans. The God who started moving on my heart didn't care what I looked like or what my fleshly desires were—He didn't judge me for being who I was or doing what I did. He *loved* me.

Well, I felt that love and I got emotional. And since I'm a man who comes from a generation that was taught to never cry, I went to the bathroom to get away from my wife and my little girl so that they wouldn't see me break. The God I met there, at "the throne" I like to say, was *not* the angry One the people at church told me so much about. I could feel His great love, and it broke me—and I hadn't cried since I was five years old, that I could remember.

That day changed my life. I said something like, "God, if You're real, come into my life and change me." And He did. He didn't change my clothes. He didn't change my occupation. I was still a musician. What did He change? My heart. That night, I went and played a show and *saw* the place I was playing in for what it really was. Before God came into my life, I thought clubs were great. But that night, I saw it like a velvet sewer. I finished my contract out in six months and then quit. Yes, that's right—I was a Christian but I was playing rock music. I started looking a little different because the booze and the drugs weren't driving me. I became faithful to my wife instantly. There was *nothing* Satan had that I wanted anymore, and I threw myself full-force into reading the Word of God.

At the time of the writing of this book, I've been preaching the Gospel of Jesus Christ for over 41 years. I've preached a lot of messages. I've written a lot of books. I'm on television stations across the world. Why? Because God had a plan for my life—and He has a plan for yours, too. His best plan starts when we let go of the lies and start not just reading the truth but living it. Let me tell you something, when God opens your eyes to the truth, there is no way you want to go back to the lies.

I've found out that the Word of God is so spiritually sound that it often tilts our natural brain. Most of us have spent our lives living only according to the five senses of this natural world. How we've been raised, what we've been taught, and what we've learned along the way in the school of hard knocks sometimes *really* gets in the way of being able to accept God's ways—which are higher than our ways and higher than some church ways, too!

This revelation that God has given me on John 14:13-14 has come at this time in my life for a reason—and if you are reading this book, I believe it's come to you for a reason, too. It's time to live the spiritual things God sent His Son, Jesus, to teach us how to live by. So, let's look at that foundational verse again.

You see, even though John 14:13-14 is overlooked as too outlandish and dismissed as too controversial, God is leading me to teach His people that *everything* that pertains to life and godliness is available to us through Jesus Christ. That means that our "everything" is included in His "ask anything"—but we cannot even come close to receiving our "everything" if we don't have the faith to believe that we are worthy enough to *ask*.

Most believers opt out of John 14:13-14, but I encourage you to opt *in*. Don't dismiss this teaching from Jesus, even if you don't understand it yet—instead, just notice exactly what that verse says and build your faith on the words of Jesus Christ:

"And whatsoever ye shall ask in My name, that will I do, that the Father may be glorified in the Son. If ye ask any thing in My name, I will do it."

Meditate on John 14:13 for a moment—remind yourself that the word *"whatsoever"* means and includes everything good. Meditate on the words *"ask," "My name,"* and *"glorified"*—and really let the words *"that will I do"* sink into your mind. As I did just this, God impressed upon me that I needed to stop focusing on asking Him for just what I *needed* and to start expanding my faith and focusing on asking Him for what I *wanted*.

> **Meditate on John 14:13 for a moment—remind yourself that the word "whatsoever" means and includes everything good.**

God revealed to me through His Word that every single answer to my prayers brought *Him* glory, and that I needed to start seeing answered prayers for what they really are—a testimony of God's goodness. That was a revelation to me, and I'll get more into the glory aspect of you being blessed later, but right now I just want you to ask yourself some questions.

Because if you don't know what you want or you feel guilty for wanting anything, well, it's hard to even approach God about it.

Are You Willing to Find Out What You Want and Why?

So, what do you really want? What *are* the desires of your heart? Have you even thought about it? Do you already know? Do you ever notice that you keep pushing them away and they keep coming back up in your heart? Are your desires primarily in one area of your life? Are they physical and deal with the health or condition of your body? Are they relationship-oriented and deal with your connections with others you know or love? Are they business or financial and deal with money, career paths, services, or things you want to experience or enjoy in life? Are they ministry-related and deal with a vision that God has given you to reach and help people in some way?

Don't let these questions pigeonhole you—search your heart and see what questions the Holy Spirit brings up to you. You might be surprised to see where you flinch and what makes you shrink back. It'll tell you a lot about where your mindset is, and where your faith in God is too. Remember that "whatsoever" means and includes *everything*. You may find that many of your desires run the gamut, or you may have just one desire pressing on your heart. Either way, write down the desire or desires that come up. Start a list. Make it plain and be specific. There is more importance than you may think in simply acknowledging your wants and taking the step of writing them down.

Then, you may want to look at what you've written and go deeper. One by one, ask yourself *why* do you want what you want? Notice what comes up. Ask yourself how will you feel when you get it? What will it settle for you *inside* of your heart? What is having "that" or doing "that" going to do for you *inside*?

Imagine how each desire being fulfilled will make you feel—will your life be more blessed because of it? How? These are just a few questions, and I encourage you to let the Holy Spirit lead you in asking yourself more. Your answers are going to reveal what you're really after if it's deeper than just "things"—and if what you want are just things, don't worry because that's OK, too!

Do You Think God Is Against You Having "Things"?

I've got a lot of "things"—people criticize me for the "things" all the time. Religious people might have a problem with things. They are so worried about "greed" that might enter your heart. But I say that if you have Christ in your heart and you put Him first, greed will *never* be an issue for you. So don't take on a religious mindset when it comes to "things." The Holy Spirit will keep you in check if you check in with the Holy Spirit, so don't worry about that! Instead of worrying about whether you'll do wrong, aim to do right. Instead of letting the lies of others convince you that you can't be trusted with "things," trust the God who trusts in you.

I mean, all you have to do is read this scripture and realize that the fears of the religious community are not God's fears: *"He that spared not His own Son, but delivered Him up for us all, how shall He not with Him also freely give us all things?"* (Romans 8:32). People act like God didn't give us His *Son.* If God will give up His own Son for us, do you think He's going to begrudge you and not give you "things"? Things are nothing compared to human life or divine life, but apparently God knows we like them enough to let us know that He will freely give them to us. Why? To enjoy. It's about joy. I'll get more into that later!

Look at what Jesus Himself said in Mark 11:24: *"Therefore I say unto you, What **things** soever ye desire, when ye pray, believe that ye receive them, and ye shall have them."* Again, trust the God who trusts in you! Remind yourself that Jesus doesn't have a problem with things as long as they don't become a master in your life. As long as the "things" don't have *you,* God is not only fine with you having things, but He *wants* you to have them. Read that verse above again and realize the obvious: Jesus wouldn't have told you to *pray* for desires if God was against desires! God just wants you to know that all good things come from Him.

Now read 1 Timothy 6:17 and see that it is God who *"giveth us richly all things to enjoy."* Are there warnings in that verse, too? *Yes,* because many people need to be warned when it comes to having money, and this verse shows us two heart issues that some people are going to have to deal with so that they don't mess up. It says, *"Charge them that are rich in this* *world, that they **be not highminded**, nor **trust** in uncertain riches, but in the living God, who giveth us richly all things to enjoy."*

Don't fall into the trap of putting something as sacred as your trust in something as "uncertain" as money. Money and things can't be trusted—but the living God can be trusted. In other words, He is alive and well and will act on your behalf according to His Word. So, expect that as you trust Him, as you extend your faith, He will be faithful to you. He will fulfill His Word and bless you as you have faith in Him.

Don't let your financial status make you high-minded. In other words, don't be an elitist who looks down your nose at those who have less—this is a warning from Jesus, and it wouldn't have been spoken if it didn't need to be heard! As believers, we need to be aware of just how wonderfully equal we are in the sight of God, regardless of our bank accounts. All of us are loved by God, and each of us deserves to be treated with dignity and respect. There are no worthless or throw-away people in God's sight.

Do You Think Someone's Value Is Tied to Their "Worth"?

I've been rich and I've been poor, and like they say…rich is better. People are nosey. They always want to know how much you've got. They use words like "worth" to determine how much you've got in the bank and the value of your assets. "What's he worth?" they ask. Whole websites are dedicated to letting nosey people know how much famous people have got—I think they make half of it up because I've seen my own name on some, and they've got it all wrong. If somebody asks me how much I'm worth, I like to tell them, "I'm worth the whole world—Jesus died for me, how much more valuable can I get?" That's not even a joke!

The bottom line when it comes to the things of God is that our worth as human beings isn't tied to our "worth" in the financial area. Just like no material thing on this planet makes a person morally better or worse, no material thing on this planet makes someone more or less valuable. Jesus died for us *all*—the very same redemptive blood flowed for rich and poor and everyone in between. The same Jesus reached out to rich and poor alike while He was on earth. He visited with all different types of people. He was a Savior to all.

We help others who are less fortunate because this is what Jesus did. We are not high-minded, because Jesus did not treat the rich one way and the poor another—He did not look down His nose on others, but instead had compassion on others. As believers, our trust is supposed to be in the Lord. To put our trust in money is always a mistake because it isn't God. Like the Word says, it is uncertain, which means unstable. It only gives the illusion of stability. Markets change, powers shift, and money's value goes up and down. However, Jesus is the same yesterday, today, and forever.

So, yes, there are those traps listed in 1 Timothy 6:17 to watch out for—but again, you won't fall into them if you just keep Jesus at the center of your life. Put God first. Let the Holy Spirit bring you to the right state of mind so that you can enjoy your blessings instead of falling into traps over your blessings. Proverbs 1:32 says prosperity destroys a fool; but you aren't a fool! You are God's child and you have the mind of Christ, not the mind of greed. Regular time spent with the Holy Spirit keeps you on track, creating a clean heart and renewing a right spirit, like Psalm 51:10 says.

Doesn't Giving Feel Good for Both the Giver and the Receiver?

I make a point to give to the poor—but I can't stand the idea of financing poverty. I preach abundance because when you just focus on meeting dire needs, you can never help anybody go any further. If God wants to grant us the desires of our heart, we have to believe it. That's why I preach the Word so that people can grab a hold of the truths that will set them free—financially as well as spiritually.

The Bible says that if you give to the poor, you lend to the Lord, and He will repay you for whatever you give (Proverbs 19:17). Jesus made giving to the poor such a habit that even when Judas went out to betray Him, everybody just assumed that Jesus had sent him out to give alms to the poor. So, it's a habit you should get into, no matter how much you have.

The best thing you can do for poor people is *not* to be poor yourself, because then you'll have way more to give. Still, no matter where you are today, start giving to the poor in some way, whether it's your finances, your time, or whatever you see that you can do to help.

I like how Jesus said not to parade around what you give to the poor—because that is degrading to people. It makes them feel terrible, and why would you want to do that? The poor have enough troubles already. They don't need anybody disrespecting them any further than the world around them already does!

Treat people with respect—*all* people. Look out for their dignity. If you do that, you'll see that just regularly giving of yourself will nip those two traps (trusting in money and high-mindedness) in the bud quickly! You can see with your very own eyes, while blessing the poor, that money in itself can't be trusted in.

A lot of those people you see on the streets weren't always poor. A lot of them have made horrible decisions or they've thought so lowly of themselves for so long that they've ended up in dire straits. Don't look down on them no matter what. Remember that it's tough to look down on the poor when you acknowledge them as real people, just like you. Show the love of God to them with honesty and give of your own substance to them on a regular basis—consider this like giving to God personally. As Jesus said, God sees even a cup of cold water when it is given.

Never forget that no matter how much or little you have, if you are a believer, you are called by God to be a giver in this world—a light in the darkness. God will provide seed for you to sow. He will increase you more and more as you give and believe His Word (Psalm 115:14). You will receive the harvest of blessing promised in the Word (2 Corinthians 9:10-11). Faith is required to receive anything from God—and every blessing received makes you that much more of a powerful influence on the earth. Giving is powerful!

As Christians, it's our duty and should be our joy to be givers in this world—we are called by God to be His hands and His feet, and to give in some way of ourselves to others regularly. We give our love, our joy, our wisdom, our time, and our finances to help others. Giving isn't just what we do; it's who we *are!*

Christians should be the greatest philanthropists on earth. All of us have something to give—and it doesn't just benefit the receiver; it also greatly benefits the giver. It feels good to everybody involved. You know, a smile is worth the world to someone whom nobody ever smiles at. A kind and uplifting word is worth a fortune to the child who never hears anything good. Mercy toward someone who never seems to get it is a great gift. And do you remember that cup of cold water Jesus talked about in Mark 9:41? Every single little thing you give as you go about your day and your life is noticed by God—and others. Every gift you give brings joy not only to God, and not only to others, but to *you.*

Don't You Think It's Time You Asked Yourself Why?

Now, I said *all* that to help you notice something about *you.* Did you notice how easy it is for you to agree with me about giving to others? Now, think about the difference you may have felt when you thought about asking God for the desires of your *own* heart. Did you notice it was easier to feel good inside when it came to *giving* but harder to feel good inside when it came to *receiving?* Did you notice a difference in how you felt about receiving needs versus receiving wants? I just want you to notice the difference, if there was one.

You see, I find that for most people, there is *no* guilt or shame or worry or fear or anything of the sort attached to giving to *others*, and there are also no problems with asking for what you need. But there are often feelings of guilt, shame, worry, or fear that arise when it comes to receiving beyond need.

If you feel uneasy about asking for what you *want*, ask yourself this question: Why? Why do you think it is that you have no problem giving to others but you suddenly have a problem with God giving to *you*? Do you think your Father in Heaven is broke...do you think He wants you to be?

Heaven is filled with nice things. Pearly gates and gold streets wouldn't even be mentioned if they didn't hold some value to God—even just for the sheer beauty of what He's built and created out of nothing. Yes, He values the souls of people above it all and you should too, but clearly He isn't choosing one or the other—He wants both. God doesn't have a problem with nice things and being surrounded by beauty, so you don't have to feel guilty if you have tangible wants. God has no problem blessing you with things, but you will have to believe that it's His will—that His Word is true, and like that verse we talked about before in Romans 8:32, that He who spared not His own Son, will indeed freely give you all things. *All* "things"!

I've got one daughter and one granddaughter—that's it. My immediate family is small. Do you think I'd enjoy seeing them broke or hurting financially? You've got to be kidding me! There is no way I want to see my wife, my child, or my grandchild hurting in any way, shape, or form whatsoever. I told my kid that I want to bless her now because I don't want her smiling at my coffin! Now, I could hoard every single dime I've got and she could just inherit my "things" when I die—but

I'd much rather see her enjoy the "things" she wants in life while I'm living. I love seeing my granddaughter with a new toy, a doll, or whatever "thing" she likes. It blesses my heart. I can't help but "freely give" to my child and my child's child. Do you think God is any other way?

God loves you. If you are made in God's image and likeness, and it brings a good feeling of joy to your heart to bless someone else, don't you think your Father also finds joy in giving to *you?* Oh, I'm here to tell you something—God gets more than just a good feeling inside when He blesses His children with answered prayers and the desires of their heart. He gets something much greater. Do you know what He gets? *Glory.* God gets glory. Read John 14:13-14 again: *"And whatsoever ye shall ask in My name, that will I do, that the Father may be **glorified** in the Son. If ye shall ask any thing in My name, I will do it."*

God is the ultimate "Good Father," just like His Son is the ultimate "Good Shepherd"—and it's when we follow Him and imitate Him as dear children that we are led to what is good in life. A good life is good all the way around—it's good spiritually, physically, and financially. Don't let anybody ever tell you differently.

CHAPTER TWO

What Does It Mean to Live a "Shall Not Want" Life?

It's all faith anyway, so I figure that I might as well believe what Jesus said—who cares what people say when you're hearing divine words that bring life? I decided long ago to choose Christ's teaching over religious people's ideas about God. If they try to tell me what God "won't do" but Jesus said something totally different, I'm going with Jesus!

My faith is not rooted in religion—I had plenty of that growing up and I've had to unlearn plenty of that since I've been born again. My faith is rooted in Jesus Christ—that is who saved me and delivered me. No man has ever done for me what Jesus has done for me. If you are saved, you can probably say the same thing. So, as I mediate on what *Jesus* said in John 14:13-14, I can clearly see that it's only a man-made, religious mindset that feels guilt for "asking" God for things.

You may want a new house, a new car, or a new job. You may want a husband or a wife. You may want a new business opportunity, all the tuition money for your kid's education, or just a new pair of shoes, or a new can of paint to color your walls to one that you want to look at every day...it doesn't matter. Big, small, or somewhere in between, I believe that God wants you to have what you want—He wouldn't have told Jesus to tell you to "ask" if it wasn't true.

There are deep heart desires and there are little things in life that we just want. Regardless, they are all included in "whatsoever," and I believe that God wants us to aim for what is best in His sight—to grow spiritually, to heal physically and emotionally, and to have "more than enough" in life to be a blessing not only to our family, but to all the families of the earth.

How can you bless everybody if you don't have enough? And how do you bless everybody in the first place?! You can bless everybody when you have more than enough for the things of everyday life, and when you sow seeds to help finance the Gospel so that *truth* can be broadcast around the world. I am a preacher, but I'm also a giver. I tithe, of course, but I give far above that because I believe in the Gospel. It has the power to save people and give them the spiritual tools to totally turn their lives around. If God could take somebody like me and turn my life around, I know that He can do it for anybody!

Look at the disciples of the Bible—those people were a mess! Did God use them? Yes, He used them. Some of them I wouldn't even hire on my staff, but look at Jesus—He turned those guys' lives around and we read their stories, their teachings, and their divine words of inspiration today. God can use anybody. The Gospel must be preached, though, because how can they hear without a preacher? And how can anybody preach unless somebody sends them? That's just the scripture! (See Romans 10:14-15.)

Abundance that will change the course of your family, your community, and even the world through the sending of the Gospel begins with you letting go of the guilt and shame surrounding "things" and money. Money isn't the root of all evil; that's the world's misquote of scripture. First Timothy 6:10 says, *"For the love of money is the root of all evil...."* As you may have heard me say before, plenty of people who don't have any money love money. But that could be another book! I trust as you read this book that you are not a lover of money but a lover of God, because all the things you want will be added to you as you seek Him and use the principles in His Word, like John 14:13-14.

Personally, I now view asking God for what I *want* in a brand-new light—one without a shred of guilt or shame. Why? Because I want to be in sync with Jesus Christ's teaching. People change, but Jesus doesn't. *"And whatsoever ye shall ask in My name, that will I do, that the Father may be glorified in the Son. If ye shall ask any thing in My name, I will do it"* is something that has totally expanded my view of what God can do. Once it does that for you, you are going to be liberated! You'll be able to start seeing yourself living a "shall not want" kind of life the Bible talks about. You'll lose the hindrance of going back and forth in your own mind. I like to say that if a double-minded man is unstable in all his ways (James 1:8), then a single-focused man of faith must be stable in all his ways. And the most single-focused Man of faith is *Jesus Christ.*

Is There Something Innately Wrong with the Desires of Your Heart?

We follow Jesus' Word because we know it's straight and true, even if it's beyond the natural, traditional way of thinking. Jesus leads us through a "narrow gate"—not a wide and destructive gate. It's not always the most traditional way but it is the most truthful way, and it requires a pure, single-focused faith.

One tradition-breaking idea is that there is something innately wrong with the desires of the believer's heart. If you are a born-again believer who consults the Word and follows the Holy Spirit within you, you don't have to be afraid of your wants—because you won't be wanting something opposed to the goodness of God. It just won't be in your heart.

There's nothing wrong with wanting nice things or wanting to do great things with the life God gave you. There's nothing wrong with receiving from God—it's what you're supposed to do. It's as important as giving. Because it's God's way to do both. There's nothing wrong with succeeding His way—in fact, there is no better way to live than His way, regardless of what you want to have or do! So don't be afraid of the desires of your own heart.

Don't listen to those who believe you can only choose one way to be—as if you have to choose between being spiritual and being blessed! Does God choose between the two when it comes to Himself? No. You don't have to choose between spirituality and material blessings. God will help you succeed at being *both* powerfully spiritual and powerfully blessed if you put Him first and apply the principles in His Word. After all, that's what they are there for!

So, as you can tell, I'm not afraid of the desires of my own heart, and I believe that you shouldn't be either. Once I got that revelation about God's goodness toward me, I stopped seeing wants as something *outside* of His will.

God has been showing me that He is *so* abundant, He is *so* loving, and He doesn't care about what people often care so much about. He uses gold for concrete. He uses precious stones on His gates. He didn't mind making sure you knew about it by putting it in His Word. In fact, He didn't flinch in saying that there are mansions in Heaven. He put it right there in the Bible. Do you know why? Because He's not religious and scared of what you think of Him for filling Heaven with an abundance of beauty. He's beyond religion. He's God, and in Him there is *zero* lack. Why do we think He somehow changes when it comes to us?

Do You Know That God Is the Planter of Good Desires?

God is the planter of desires in the heart of the believer—and what He plants is not meant for harm, but for good. Again, bringing those desires to pass isn't just a blessing for the receiver, but a glorification of God for all who see it. I just can't say that enough!

Once you know in your heart that God is for you and not against you, and that your heart's desires are not only His will but His wish for you, well, your faith just rises up easier—you understand His love in a greater way because you see Him as a good Father.

Jesus wasn't called the Good Shepherd for nothing! If He goes out of His way to save and rescue just one lost sheep, will

He neglect and forget about the rest of His flock? No. He is a Good Shepherd who will not only tend to His flock, but generously care and love each and every one following His lead (Matthew 18:11-14).

If you don't follow Jesus' lead when it comes to your desires, you can't get what He has for you, which are only good things—good desires come out of a good heart. So then you have to ask yourself, are my desires good? Is there anything innately wrong with wanting a new home, a new car, or a new pair of shoes? Is there anything innately wrong with wanting a good business, a good spouse, a good dinner out on the town? Is there anything innately wrong with wanting to have more than enough for your children and your children's children? Is there anything innately wrong with wanting to be a benefactor to someone or to greatly support foundations and ministries that do good in the world? The answer to all of that is "*no.*"

If you worry about a desire, just run it by the Lord. He has saved you, His Spirit is in you, and He will help you to realize that whatever you want isn't innately wrong if it's good. You can feel confident that He *is* the Good Shepherd and He will never, ever lead you astray—not even when it comes to the deep desires of your heart or the little and big wants you have in life either. Again, God is the planter of those desires. He's not against you; He's for you. If you live well, don't you want your kids living well? If you're living your dreams, don't you want to see your friends, your coworkers, and all your loved ones living theirs, too?

Never forget that the blood of Jesus has washed you clean—pure and white as snow on the inside, where it matters! The Holy Spirit is now dwelling inside of you, helping you to live your life God's way, and that means Christ is guiding you. And if you allow Him the opportunity, He will guide you throughout your life. So, be confident that He loves you enough to bless you. That acceptance of His love and His stamp of approval on you creates a more open-hearted way of praying—it helps the energy of faith rise up out of your heart to God's ears.

> You were made for a "shall not want" and "wanting nothing" kind of life—because that's the abundant life, which Jesus said in John 10:10 that He came to give.

You were made for a "shall not want" and "wanting nothing" kind of life—because that's the abundant life, which Jesus said in John 10:10 that He came to give. He didn't just come to give it to somebody else; He came to give it to you, too. But what does it even mean? Does it mean wanting nothing at all—as in not having desires?

Is "Shall Not Want" About Wanting Nothing at All?

"The Lord is my Shepherd; I shall not want" has got to be one of the most famous passages. Those few words from Psalm 23:1 have been said and read so much, many people don't even bother thinking about what they mean. I like to call God's overwhelming blessings the "shall not want" life. To me (in light of Christ's teaching in John 14:13-14 that is the main

theme of this book), those aren't just a bunch of flowery words. "Shall not want" actually means something powerful.

Does it mean that you "shall not want" because you are so spiritual and separated from earthly life that you don't want anything at all anymore? No. We all want something, even if we say we don't. Even *God* wants something—*you!* He obviously wanted Heaven as His home too, gold streets and all. Not wanting anything may seem spiritual, but it's not. It's just denial of being a human being created in God's image. We all want something.

So how do you end up at a place of wanting nothing? You end up at "I shall not want" when you follow the *Shepherd*, which is Jesus Christ. And in following Jesus Christ and His teachings, you learn how to receive what you want. Spiritual wants. Physical wants. Financial wants. Any kind of want that is good in His sight is available by following the Shepherd, Jesus Christ.

When you "ask" in prayer, ask in faith. Ask as if Jesus is right here on the earth, looking into your eyes like He looked into the eyes of those in biblical times long ago—listening and responding to you, and saying just what He told so many others: *"According to your faith be it unto you"* (Matthew 9:29). Expect to get what you want. Remember, your faith in Jesus' words is needed to get what you want!

God has given us principles in His Word to help us on our journey through life. It's an economic world. We've been given a physical body. We have the desire to connect with others and find joy in relationships. As believers, we *choose* to be guided by the Word of God and the Holy Spirit within us—both of whom desire to lead us to a place of "I shall not want" because God has "richly given me all things to enjoy."

Yes, there are many challenges to overcome, but there is a *lot* of joy and triumph to be had as we live our life. Having a Psalm 23 "I shall not want" state of mind is wonderful. It's a whole lot better than living with a mind full of worry and doubt and the cycle of lack that follows.

Every day, in some way—spiritually, physically, financially, or in any other area I am focusing on—God is giving me what I want as I stretch my faith and obey His Word. I'm not being arrogant. This isn't about arrogance; it's about assurance in my God and the teachings of His Son!

God doesn't just drop what I want in my lap without anything done on my part. Although God does sometimes surprise me without me having to say a word, I am the one who has to conform to the principles of the Word and do them. I have to discipline my thoughts when the natural mind wants to trump the spirit or when circumstances seem to be going against what I want. I have to use my authority in Christ, look beyond natural circumstances, and choose to speak the Word.

I have to "say unto the mountain" as Jesus said, and focus my thoughts, words, and energy on what I *want*. I'm the one who has to decide if I'm going to give myself permission to use my imagination, dream, and believe that what Jesus said is actually true—even if everybody else dismisses it.

When we read the Word, we have a choice to believe it or not. When we pray, we choose what words we are going to say. As we live, day by day and in every situation that comes up, we are the ones who choose for ourselves if we want to live in accordance with the Word of God or not.

God is good. He loves us. He didn't give us life just so we can endure it—He sent His Son to give us abundant life (John 10:10). For too long we've thought the opposite, but I believe that no matter what you've been told or how you feel today, God is *not* afraid of what is in your heart. It's time to expand our view of what God can do. It's time to live with more faith and less doubt and stress. It's time to believe that what Jesus said about "asking" is *true*.

Do You Have a Problem with Feeling Loved?

How much of your "best life" are you willing to believe God for? Do you think God loves you enough to bring it to pass? Do you love yourself enough to even expect to receive? For many, the answers to these kinds of questions lie in an acceptance of the purity of God's love.

God's love is not a "little kind of love" but is so big that it encompasses all that He is. It's a love that is immeasurable. In fact, God's love is the driving force behind all His promises to bless you.

> *Nay, in all these things we are **more than conquerors** through Him that **loved us**. For I am persuaded, that neither death, nor life, nor angels, nor principalities, nor powers, nor things present, nor things to come, nor height, nor depth, nor any other creature, **shall be able to separate us from the love of God**, which is in Christ Jesus our Lord.*
>
> Romans 8:37-39

Love is what God has for you. Remember that when your knees hit the floor—don't talk to Him like He's an abusive Father who wants to hold out on you just to make you squirm. That is a lie from the enemy. Don't look at yourself in the mirror and cut down what you see—what you're looking at is someone God made and loves. It hurts Him if you don't appreciate His creation. *You* are His creation. He sent His Son to die for you. Believe that He loves you. Even if you have never been loved once in your life.

I didn't feel loved as a kid—so what! I've got all the love in the world now. Jesus came! God came down in the flesh for me. He did it for me, just like He did it for you. The love of God pushes out all sorts of junk the devil tries to throw into our minds. The love of God destroys lies. You aren't alone. You've got all of Christendom behind you—a family bigger than you know. Some are here on earth; others are in Heaven. Guess what? God loves every single one of us, including you.

God doesn't love the apostle Paul more than you. He doesn't love one saint more than you. He loves us *all*. He's not a respecter of persons…but He is a respecter of faith. His love doesn't change. But if you want your life to change, you have to use the currency He chose, which is faith. By faith, you know that you are saved. By faith, you need to know that you are loved. Jesus sent the Holy Spirit after He rose from the dead for a reason—and one of them was so that *you* would have a Comforter. The Holy Spirit fills you, and if you stick with Him in prayer, the love of the Father will come pouring out of His Spirit into you. You won't just know you're loved; you'll feel the love!

YOUR EVERYTHING IS HIS ANYTHING

So, when you bow your heart and bend your knees in prayer like all the saints who came before you, you will not be fearful. You will recognize that it is Love alone that reached out to you, it's Love alone that saved you, and that there is absolutely *nothing* that can separate you from the Love that *is* our God.

*For this cause I bow my knees unto the Father of our Lord Jesus Christ, Of whom the whole family in Heaven and earth is named, that He would grant you, according to the riches of His glory, to be strengthened with might by His Spirit in the inner man; That Christ may dwell in your hearts by faith; that ye, being rooted and grounded in love, May **be able to comprehend** with all saints what is the breadth, and length, and depth, and height; And **to know the love of Christ**, which passeth knowledge, that ye might **be filled with all the fulness of God**. Now unto Him that is **able to do exceeding abundantly above all that we ask or think**, according to the **power that worketh in us**.*

Ephesians 3:14-20

To realize your visions and dreams, to have faith that moves mountains, and to have the confident bravery to ask God for what you want, you must accept God's pure love and pure goodness toward *you* as a matter-of-fact thing.

To know the love of Christ is the beginning of being filled with all the fullness of God. He *is* able to do more than we ask or think, but it is only in relation to the amount of His power that we *allow* to work within us. We choose how much of His love we accept. We choose how much of His Word we believe.

We choose how much of His power we want to work through us and in us.

Do You Limit God's Love in Your Own Mind?

Limits. Capacity. Love. Often, at the heart of a believer's concern about whether a teaching from Christ is true is a deep doubt about God's *capacity* to love. Asking for what you want and expecting divine results takes childlike faith in not only what Jesus taught but also in the truth that God loves *you*—and He loves *you* enough to give you what you've asked in His Son's name.

As believers, we are *in* this world but not *of* this world—our first home is Heaven, and our first and last Father is God. That means when we read the Word of God, we can have faith like little children, even if everything or everyone around us is increasingly skeptical and doubtful, because we know that natural laws are often blown away for us by our Father. We serve a miracle-working God. We serve a Father who loves us, but requires that we step up to the plate and believe in that love and believe in His Word.

If we limit the love of God in our own mind, we also limit our ability to *receive*. Imagine God reaching out to you with an answer to your prayer, but you choose to push Him away because you don't believe He loves you enough to answer—that is what many believers do when they doubt God's love.

When believers doubt God loves them enough to do what He said, they are really doubting His very nature, which is love. How can we receive from a Father we don't allow ourselves to believe really loves us? How can we receive an answer when we push Him away in our own mind and heart? We must have faith in the love of God. Sometimes this is hard if you haven't had much purity in love during your life, but it's to your benefit to start seeing God in the light of His love. Your faith works by love, so if this is an issue for you, I encourage you to start speaking scriptures that focus on the love of God over yourself.

Don't let life's past experiences with *people* diminish the reality of God's divine love for you. Your future in Him is loving, no matter who did what to you in your past. Learning to accept His limitless love is a key to unlocking your own faith in the promises of God. You cannot trust someone whom you do not believe loves you and has your best interests at heart. So, get rid of those old thoughts. Replace them with the words of truth in the scriptures so that you can, without doubt, believe that everything Jesus said you can have, you can have!

Can You Take the Heat for What You Believe?

There are many financial principles I believe because Jesus said them, and I believe that God loves me enough to fulfill His Word. Take the hundredfold return principle, for instance. Many people don't believe this and actually preach against it, even though Jesus said it. They excuse it away, in one way or another. I don't, but I do preach something many others don't when it comes to the hundredfold return—persecution. In Mark 10:30, Jesus tells us that those who give up everything for the sake of the Gospel can expect a hundredfold return on what they gave up, but that big, giant blessing comes with persecution: *"But he shall receive an hundredfold now in this time, houses, and brethren, and sisters, and mothers, and children, and lands, **with persecutions**; and in the world to come eternal life."*

Not everyone is called to give up all for the Gospel's sake. Not everyone can receive the hundredfold return, because they do not believe it. (It's yet another one of Jesus Christ's controversial but true statements that tilt the human mind.) It's also true that not everyone can take the heat for receiving the blessing. Many people just don't want the persecution. They'd rather give up the blessing than endure the heat of other people's scorn.

The principle of "taking the heat" for God's blessings remains important, no matter if you are a minister or a layperson—because the truth is that there is always going to be somebody who doesn't like it when you succeed God's way. There's always someone who wants to tear down those whom God raises up, and they seem to enjoy doing it.

You just have to decide that you don't care what others say if God's Word says something different. God's plan for your life is worth whatever "heat" you have to take for having it. Being blessed nearly always comes with some kind of persecution, but once you know that, it doesn't blindside you so much when it comes. You can see it for what it is—an attack on God's goodness and an attack on the glory God will get when others see you blessed by His hand. So, decide today that you are willing to take the heat. Decide that the blessing is worth it— and not only for you, but for all who will hear the testimony and reach out in faith to God, too, because they heard about what God has done for you. God's glory is at stake.

Can You Let Go of the Lies and Hold On to the Truth?

I'm the kind of man who is willing to take persecution for the sake of what I believe. I don't like persecution. Who likes it? Nobody likes it! But will I abandon the Word? Will I abandon the dictates of my own conscience and heart just to avoid persecution? Will I rob God of His glory just to bow down to some attack from the enemy? No way! Not me! I will not. I don't back down if I believe God has told me something, or shown me something, or given me something—and I especially don't back down when I know He wants me to preach something that will bring Him glory in the end.

I believe that you've got to get like a bulldog in holding on to what you believe in your heart—regardless of the naysayers. That's why asking yourself questions about what you want and why you want it is so important. That's why letting the Holy Spirit and the Word guide you is so important. You need to know what you believe and what you want. You need be secure in God's goodness and His love toward you enough to be able to believe Jesus' teachings like a little child. Remember, you may have years of thinking the opposite from God's Word drilled into your mind—and those wrong ideas about God and what He wants for you really need to be exposed for what they are, *wrong*, and let go of so that you can move forward in truth.

Just like you can't move forward while holding on to the past, you can't walk in God's truth while holding on to a lie from the enemy. You've got to be able to let those lies go. Remember that just because something is traditional does not mean that it's true—I don't care how many times it gets repeated, lack is not God's will for you in any area of your life. There is no lack in Heaven and Jesus told us, in what is known as The Lord's Prayer, to pray that God's will be done *"in earth, as it is in Heaven"* (Matthew 6:10).

Jesus also plainly stated that He came to give us life and life more abundantly (John 10:10). That's not just about tangible things, though it includes that if you want that— it's about everything. More peace. More love. More power in every way. More answers to prayers that bring about an abundant state of being—spiritually, physically, financially, and in every other way.

Realize that it's your faith in God's abundant Word that draws blessings into your life. It will all be done according to your faith. So, it's time to believe that you *can* have an abundant life—a gloriously good life in every way—and it's time to feel good about *asking* for it because you know that God loves you and is faithful.

Can you see yourself in a "shall not want" and "wanting nothing" life? Can you have that kind of experience here on earth? Yes, you can, and I believe that you will. Don't let religious tradition or man-made ideas steal the revealed truth in the words of Jesus from your heart. Protect them. Some people may not be able to handle it, so don't cast your pearls before swine that will only trample what is in your heart (Matthew 7:6). Choose to hold on to what you believe and do it with joy.

Jesus is the Way, the Truth, and the Life for *you*—let others say what they will. Just lean on His love and on His power. Use His teachings. Realize that God's Word is filled with stories of God superseding natural ways of doing things in order to bring spiritual, physical, and even financial abundance into the lives of His children. We get what we believe for. So, if God has done it before, He can do it again—and He can do it for you and through you! Your everything is His anything, and your "wanting nothing" blessings will one day be a testimony of God's goodness for all the world to see.

CHAPTER THREE

Do You Realize the Power of Jesus' Name?

"Let this mind be in you, which was also in Christ Jesus: who, being in the form of God, thought it not robbery to be equal with God: but made himself of no reputation, and took upon him the form of a servant, and was made in the likeness of men: and being found in fashion as a man, he humbled himself, and became obedient unto death, even the death of the cross. **Wherefore God also hath highly exalted him, and given him a name which is above every name: that at the name of Jesus every knee should bow, of things in heaven, and things in earth, and things under the earth; and that every tongue should confess that Jesus Christ is Lord, to the glory of God the Father.***"*

Philippians 2:5-11

Whose name has God exalted above *all* other names? *Jesus Christ.* Everything in *Heaven*, everything in *earth*, and everything *under earth* will one day bow to one name—whose name? *Jesus Christ.* One day every tongue will confess only One as Lord—who will that be? *Jesus Christ.*

There is a *reason* we have been told to put our prayers in that name—because that name doesn't just stand for something, it stands for Someone. Someone whom God chose to come, take on the likeness of men, and die for the sins of the world. God is the Supreme Power over all, and He has given all power and all authority—over things in *Heaven*, things *in* the earth, and even things *under* the earth—to His only begotten Son, *Jesus Christ*. This means that there is no life that has ever existed, or ever will exist, that is immune to the divine power of Jesus Christ or exists outside of the divine authority of Jesus Christ.

The name of Jesus will endure forever, and like it or not, even the demons recognize Jesus Christ as God's choice—and they fear the Ultimate Power that backs up His holy name. You see, when the God of all Creation makes a choice, it doesn't matter who believes it's true or not—it's true because God said it. Our belief doesn't create God's truth. God's truth exists and persists whether we acknowledge and receive it or deny and reject it. As believers, we are by our very name followers of Christ. We are Christians, which means we have accepted God's choice and God's truth—and now, that means we have the right to use the name of Jesus when we pray.

When we begin to understand the power of who we serve, we begin to understand the power behind the name. Don't ever get so accustomed to saying the name of Jesus that you forget just *who* you are talking about!

So, when Jesus said, *"And whatsoever ye shall ask **in My name**, that will I do, that the Father may be glorified in the Son. If ye shall ask any thing **in My name**, I will do it"* (John 14:13-14), He was giving *you* permission to not only *ask* God for "whatsoever" you desire, but He was giving *you* permission to use His name.

Jesus—He Is Called Wonderful, Our Counsellor in All

One of the most telling scriptures about His name is in Isaiah 9:6, where there is a prophecy that tells us what Jesus would be called: *"and His name shall be called **Wonderful, Counsellor,** The **mighty God,** The **everlasting Father,** The **Prince of Peace.**"* Jesus and His Father are One.

Jesus Christ is called Wonderful for a reason—because who He is and what He does is wonderful. If you ask for bread, He will not give you a stone. If you ask for a fish, he will not give you a snake. Jesus said it best in Matthew 7:11, *"If ye then, being evil, know how to give good gifts unto your children, how much more shall your Father which is in Heaven give good things to them that ask Him?"*

Don't let anyone lie to you and tell you that Jesus is not wonderful. His ministry was marked by goodness, grace, mercy, love, and truth above all. He was a rescuer of souls then; He is a rescuer of souls now. Jesus didn't go around putting sickness and disease on people in His earthly ministry, and He does not put sickness and disease on people now from His place at the right hand of the Father in Heaven. He was a Healer then; He is a Healer now, and it's wonderful.

Jesus did all sorts of miracles in His earthly ministry. He went above and beyond to provide for His followers physically during His earthly ministry—which means He was a provider then, and guess what? He is a provider now, too! Jesus dispensed wisdom that blew people away during His time here on earth, and His wisdom is still blowing us away today—He has not changed. And if anyone lacks wisdom, James 1:5 says to do what? *Ask!* It says God will liberally give it to you if you ask. So, ask! Neither the Father nor the Son enjoy seeing you hurt or stumbling through life—they are wonderful and are available to those who have the guts to seek, ask, and knock (Matthew 7:7-8).

I could go down a looong list of all the wonderful things Jesus did during His earthly ministry, but the point is that everything He did and everything He was then, He is still doing and being today. Jesus was wonderful then and He is wonderful now. Get rid of any doubt that Jesus is anything less than wonderful!

Jesus Christ is also called the Counsellor—so realize that you will only get good and solid wisdom and guidance from Him. He will not lead you astray. He will shine a light onto your path, draw you to walk with Him in faith, and only give you advice that is in line with His Word. He says "My sheep know my voice, and a stranger they will not follow"—which means you can always count on the still, small voice of His Spirit that is speaking to your heart to be in line with Jesus' words and His nature.

The Counsellor will not guide you to destruction; He will only guide you to life, and that means *abundant* life! So, when you ask for "whatsoever" you desire, realize that the Source giving it to you is Jesus, and He is wiser than any other. Trust His wisdom knowing that He will honor you and bless you, and He will do it in His timing, which is always the right timing. If you experience a delay, know this: a delay is not a denial.

Don't bend to the pressure of time. Don't relinquish your faith too early. Choose instead *not* to get weary in well doing, knowing that you will reap if you do not faint in your faith, according to Galatians 6:9. Choose not to fall into laziness either knowing that, like Hebrews 6:12 says, it is through two things—faith and patience—that you will inherit the promises of God. Patience is not giving up; it's standing and continuing to stand. It's moving forward in faith, with joy, until you receive exactly what you want.

Jesus—He Is Called Mighty and Everlasting

Jesus is called the mighty God in Isaiah 9:6 because He is *not* weak. He is more than able to do whatever He said He would do! He can also make sovereign choices if He so desires. Of course, He will never break His Word—He's bound Himself to His own Word—but He can go above and beyond it if He chooses. Take Paul on the road to Damascus, for instance.

Jesus literally appeared to Paul on the road to Damascus out of thin air and asked him some pretty pointed questions in order to talk some sense into the man—go read it for yourself in Acts chapter nine. Paul was a hard and cruel persecutor of Christians, and yet Jesus divinely intervened with a supernatural event. Before you know it, Paul sees the light. He converts to Christianity, stops persecuting, and starts preaching. His life is totally turned around and he becomes the writer of two-thirds of the New Testament. You see, Paul was Jesus Christ's choice for that job, and Jesus wasn't opposed to going above and beyond to reach him.

While there is nowhere in the Bible that promises Jesus will go above and beyond His Word, we can see by this example that He does sometimes do unusual things to make sure His will is done. That is His sovereign right. Jesus is not weak—He's *mighty*. Do not underestimate His power! Don't even allow yourself to think He can't do what He said. The same power that brings His promises to pass is the same power that heals, work miracles, saves, and touches people's lives every day. It's the same power that will go totally above and beyond to get things done, if He wills. Glory! You serve a Mighty God, and His name is Jesus! Don't even let yourself think any differently.

Jesus is also called the everlasting Father. Why? Because the Son is One with the Father. And doesn't it give you even greater security while calling on the name of Jesus to know that He's never going away?

Everything you see today will one day fade away. Life is a vapor. Cities and societies come and go. Jesus is an everlasting constant among this change—because He existed before the foundations of the world. Jesus remains the same yesterday, today, and forever (Hebrews 13:8). And that means when we pray and use His name, we aren't dealing with Someone temporary—we are dealing with Someone whose abundant life is eternal. That means His abundance toward us will never end. It will always bring glory to God when we are blessed spiritually, physically, or financially. Oh, I'm enjoying writing this! I hope you are enjoying reading it.

Jesus—He Is Called the Prince of Peace, Not Anxiety

Jesus is *not* called the Prince of Anxiety, the Prince of Fear, or even the Prince of War. Jesus is called the Prince of Peace. Many Christians are scared to believe Jesus' teaching—*"And whatsoever ye shall ask in My name, that will I do, that the Father may be glorified in the Son. If ye shall ask any thing in My name, I will do it"* (John 14:13-14)—because they are filled with anxiety and fear waging an inner war within their own minds that steals their peace.

The good news is that Jesus is the restorer of peace—and peace begins inside our heart first. The "peace that passes all understanding" that the scripture speaks of begins to affect our everyday lives only after we are first experiencing it in our hearts and minds. We aren't robots, and our behavior often changes according to our emotions. God made us emotional beings. Jesus is compassionate in this, but strong in sharing His truth—because the truth that you *know* is the truth that sets you free.

It's not just a crying shoulder that will bring you real peace. It's not a commiserating friend or a misery-loves-company buddy who will give you peace. No matter how much you overthink, you cannot gain real peace for your mind by ruminating—life does not work that way. The truth is that Jesus is the Prince of Peace, and that makes seeking Him, believing Him, and receiving from Him the Answer to having real peace. His Word is the truth, and the truth you know will set you free—so ask yourself, "Do I *know* it?" Faith is knowing it.

Faith is not just intellectually "knowing it." There are plenty of people who know the scriptures but don't believe them at all, and so have zero results because they don't believe or apply them. Faith is knowing it in your heart. It's childlike. The greatest truth in the Bible, to me, is John 3:16. This is my paraphrase, but it's the verse that says that God loved the world so much that He *gave* us Jesus, so that whoever would just believe on Him wouldn't perish, but have everlasting life. It's an eternal mindset that will help you see how the Prince of Peace rules and reigns—He begins by making peace in you. There can be no outer peace without inner peace.

When you ask for "whatsoever" you desire, expect to get it—not from a place of worry and anxiety, but from an inner place of peace. Your level of peace will often correlate with your level of faith. Anxiety-praying may be an emotional, temporary state of the mind, but you don't have to remain there—the Prince of Peace resides in you. He will lift you right out of that state of mind and give you the strength and power you need to speak His Word, use His name, and pull down strongholds of the enemy. He will endue you with power from on high so that you can read the Word with boldness—and the more Word you meditate on (hearing, and hearing by the Word), the more faith you will build in that Word (2 Corinthians 10:3-5; Luke 24:49; Romans 10:17).

You see, when you allow the Prince of Peace to become your peace, you will find it so easy to take that permission slip He gave you to use His name—to *ask* in His name knowing that He will do it (John 14:13-14)!

All of these names that we call Jesus are just a fraction of who He is—and yet we have been given permission to use His holy name. When we pray in His name, we can expect results. So, it's time we take off the limits. If "whatsoever" means everything, and if our everything is included in His encouragement to "ask anything"…well, what are we waiting for?

If Jesus Is So Powerful, Why Give the Devil So Much Energy?

When Jesus came down in the flesh to live as a man, to die, and to give Himself up as a sacrifice for mankind, He completely and forever established our authority over the natural world—which means we also have authority over the devil and all his works (1 John 3:8).

We don't need to ask God to get rid of the devil for us. We need to enforce our authority as believers by using the name of Jesus to get rid of the devil and all his works. Anything that might be trying to steal our blessings or buck our blood-bought authority isn't half as powerful as Jesus.

Remember that the devil is a thief who comes to steal, to kill, and to destroy—but again, Jesus came to give us life and life in abundance (John 10:10). If we want abundance in life, we can expect the devil to sometimes try to hinder. Who cares? We have the name of Jesus. This is not la-la land where we should be surprised when the devil attacks believers; it's earth, and the devil is just a rogue angel, fallen and destitute of all spiritual authority.

The devil convinced one-third of the angels to follow him and they were thrown out of Heaven along with him (Revelation 12:4,9). So, yes, he's got a third of Heaven who are also just as sick and disturbed as he is. So what! The spiritual reality is that all he and the rest of his angelic losers really have is a "roaring lion" act—that's what they regularly try to use to intimidate God's people. They deal in the realm of the senses. They know human weaknesses very well because, let's face it, they've been around a while!

The devil has no new tricks though, and you can be certain that the same temptations he used back in Bible days are the same ones he uses today. Don't let it bother you. Don't give him so much credit or concern. Don't waste your energy. In fact, the less energy, attention, frustration, and glory you give to that idiot, the better off you'll be!

Look, there is more power in Jesus' thumbnail than in the whole lot of those fallen fools. So when you think about who is stealing, killing, and destroying things in your own life, I want you to imagine how small the devil really is…and how *big* the God *you* serve is. The Bible says that one day, we're all going to see him and say something like, "*This?* This is what fooled the whole world?! You've got to be kidding me!" (See Isaiah 14:12-17.)

Yes, the devil is very dramatic. Yes, he tries so much to get you in fear and to look at the natural—to believe that God doesn't care, or that you don't have any power, or that you just have to take whatever comes down the pipe in life. Just remember that as sure as the natural world exists, the spiritual world exists too, and you serve the Winner! Eternally, you will win. And you can win here, too. You have the name of Jesus, and you have the permission, authority, and blessing to use it. All things in Heaven, in earth, and under the earth have to stand down when you use His name in faith.

Do You Know That Challenge by Challenge, You Can Win?

Don't let the devil use your emotions to take you for a ride—you are part of a group, the same one I'm in, called the Body and Bride of Christ. We are not people who are only moved by the senses. We are people who are moved by our *faith*. Our eyes are opened. Our faith is strong. There are more with us than with them—because *Jesus Christ* is with us, backing us, urging us to use His name and to focus on "asking" for "whatsoever" we desire from God. We live from faith to faith and victory to victory.

Are there challenges? Of course. The devil is alive. He's spiritually dead, but still moving around complicating things. But his day is coming! Until that day, we still get lots of opportunities to enforce his defeat, overcome circumstances that pop up, and receive what we desire in life. Guess what? No matter what happens, you should think like this: "Challenge by challenge, I win! I don't care what it looks like. I don't go by what I see; I go by what I believe—and I believe Jesus!"

If you need wisdom, ask for it. Ask the Holy Spirit to open your

> **There are more with us than with them—because Jesus Christ is with us, backing us, urging us to use His name and to focus on "asking" for "whatsoever" we desire from God. We live from faith to faith and victory to victory.**

57

spiritual eyes to the big-picture reality that you are the winner because you serve the Winner. It will help you to think clearly about temporary problems when you recognize your eternal victory. Make sure you are hearing, and hearing the Word, especially during a challenge, so that your faith can surge strongly—so that you don't shy away from asking and receiving everything you want from the Lord.

Asking is all over the Bible—but so few do it with very much faith. Look at Jesus' words in Matthew 7:7 and I challenge you to do it. *Ask* in faith, knowing you will receive. *Seek* in faith, knowing you will find. *Knock* in faith, knowing the door will open for you. This passage is about salvation, but it's not just about salvation—it's about *everything* you desire from the Lord. Faith is a requirement.

If Your Life Is Precious to God, Why Isn't It to You?

Everyone, to a degree, believes that their life is precious because most don't want to die! But every day in life, believers do things that demonstrate the opposite—they *don't* think their life is very important. Nothing could be further from the truth.

We are spirit beings first—this is a miracle. We are spirit beings housed in flesh. Even the angels aren't as important in God's eyes as we are, and He literally put us in rank just a little lower than Himself (Psalm 8:4-6 AMPC). That's how precious a human being is to God.

Look around and you will see that the planet He gave us is beautiful—far more beautiful than any other sphere spinning in the cosmos that we can see. Heaven will be even better! But earth, if you really have eyes to see, is likely a close second! This place was intended to be paradise—and it's nobody's fault but our own that it's gotten to the state in which it is today. Still, the birds sing every morning. The earth teems with life, a force of life that continually pushes forward to new life over and over again.

We are precious in God's sight—made in His image and likeness. And just like God has separated Himself into three (Father, Son, and Holy Spirit), He has created us as a pattern of three as well. We are spirits who have a soul, and we are housed in a body. The soul is the mind, will, and emotions—it's not the same thing as your brain. Our mind learns, grows, adapts, and changes according to what we hear, what we experience, what we encounter, and what we believe, so why not give ourselves the gift of truth and power? Why *not* develop the mind of Christ, which means an "anointed" mind?

We need to recognize that if our life, if our mind, and if our body is precious to God, then it should be precious to us—and it's our job to honor it and take care of who we are and what we've been given.

The more we recognize our power grows by feeding our faith and doing it, the greater our lives will be. This body is an earth suit that we will one day shed, but that doesn't mean it's not precious or valuable. It just means it's temporary and rare! There is only one of you. There will only ever be one of you! It's important for you to see your spirit as the "primary you"—who you really are—and to develop your mind in the things of God so that you can live out of your spirit more than your flesh.

You are loved by God. So, if the life He's given you is precious to Him, it must also be precious to you, too. Don't sell yourself short!

God or "Them"—Who Are You Going to Believe?

While life's experiences may have told you not to expect much, or to expect bad things, God says don't think that way— because your faith and your anointed mind (the mind of Christ working in you) can change *all* of that.

The natural world's way of thinking is almost always in opposition to spiritual thinking. When they say, "Don't expect much," God says, "Expect more." When they say, "That's impossible," God says, "All things are possible with Me." When they say, "You'll never be able to have that, or do that, or be that," God says, "You can have whatsoever you say, you can do all things through Christ who gives you strength because you are My child and all things are possible for you." When they say, "I doubt that," God says, "Have faith in Me."

You just have to ask yourself—who are you going to believe? I suggest the Lord. Stop reining in your dreams, visions, goals, and ideas—start expanding them out. Stop listening to those whose only source of information is this earthly experience. You serve the Lord, and He is heavenly! That means He sees things from a liiiiitle bit of a higher vantage point.

Stop listening to what you "can't do" or "can't have"—because who are "they" who are saying those things anyway? What do they know? All they can tell you is what they think or what they've seen in the natural, which means they can't tell you your future—they can only predict according to their own past! They can't tell you who you *are*, but God can. God knows exactly who you are and what you are capable of with Him. So, if He said you can ask and receive, then you can! If He said you can *have*, you can *do*, and you can *be*, then you can. Period. End of statement.

There is no need to mentally cut yourself off from what the Word has promised to you—abundant life. There is no need to restrict yourself from having God's best—not in your mind, not in your heart, and not in your prayer life. Jesus did not come to condemn you but to save you, and I believe to save you in every way that you need it. Using His name is part of the plan. You use it when you gain spiritual salvation, but you will need to use it for other promises in the Word, too.

You have *all* the *power* you need because you have the Holy Spirit dwelling within you. You have *all* the *authority* you need because Jesus has given you permission to use His name to get things done. From the spirit world to the natural world, you can use the name of Jesus and see your needs met, your desires fulfilled, and you bring glory to the Father in the process.

Anything and *everything* is wrapped up in His holy name. Through faith and use of the power Jesus has given, you can live in real peace, real joy, and spiritual, physical, and financial prosperity in this life. Do you want God's best enough to ask for it? I pray that you do! There is no better way to pray than to do it His way—by asking in faith and using His holy name.

CHAPTER FOUR

Why Not Give God Glory?

What happens if you *don't* listen to what Jesus said and you *don't* ask God for anything in Jesus' name? The obvious but hard-to-hear truth is this: God *won't* be glorified in the earth through *you*. Now, I know that is strong, but take a look at John 14:13-14 again:

> *And whatsoever ye shall ask in My name, that will I do,* ***that the Father may be glorified in the Son.*** *If ye shall ask any thing in My name, I will do it.*

If you choose *not* to rely on the Lord and choose not to ask in faith, and consequently don't receive, you not only lose out on what Christ wanted to do for you, but you also cheat the Father out of the glory He would have gotten if you'd had the guts to obey and have some faith. Oh, again, I know that's strong! It stings a little, but it is true.

You can't get away from the fact that whether you realize it or not, you are giving glory to something or someone every day. It can be as simple as when you talk about the problems more than the answers—in that case, you're glorifying the problems. It can be as simple as when you say, "Yeaaaah, but…" in response to one of Christ's teachings—in that case, you're glorifying your doubt that His Word is true more than you're glorifying the teaching.

It takes faith to step out and ask for big things. It takes courage to look at your life and decide you want better. It's very humbling to your pride to put your faith in God. It means that you recognize that God is bigger than you are, and that you cannot do or receive all that you want on your own. It means that you must not only recognize His love for you, but also His ability to do anything through *you*—and there is a certain calming effect with having faith in God. It's peaceful when you realize that *you* aren't the one who's going to solely make things happen.

Do You Use the Imagination God Gave You?

Life is more fulfilling when you are moving in the direction of your dreams and bringing God glory. The energy of faith moves things around in the spirit realm, which affects the natural realm. Every day, with every thought, word, and action you make, you are drawing in what you want to you and pushing away what you don't want.

Imagination is a gift from God—it's not just for children. Along with prayer, imagination helps you to see what's in your own heart. What comes out when you dream? What comes up when you pray?

If you *don't* take a look inside yourself, if you *don't* use the imagination God gave you, and if you *don't* acknowledge what you really want and then *ask* God for it, you are really missing out. You're missing out on the excitement of living by faith, on the joy of seeing your heart's desires come to pass, and on the glory God will get when you share your testimony and what you've learned with others.

It's all about what *you* do with what *He* has said. Believers are powerful when they *believe* because, unlike *un*believers, we are putting our faith in the timeless, living, and active Word of God. No positive affirmation in the world can compete with any statement based on God's Word—His words are divine and they have more power and more authority. You alone are powerful and can do great things, of course, but by humbling yourself before God and applying the teachings of Jesus Christ, you'll do even *greater* things.

The biggest blessing is that you'll have more peace and joy in the process of using your imagination, asking God for what you want, and moving in the direction of that desire through the actions you take every day.

Do You Know That the Source Is the One Who Gets the Glory?

Do you ever notice how many people talk about "burn out" as they are trying to get what they want in life? Even preachers talk about it. The problem is that it comes out of a secular mindset that sees itself as the only real source of "making things happen." God never burns you out. If you're a believer and you're burning out, you're taking on a burden He didn't give you—trying to do it all on your own, as if nothing will happen unless you make it happen.

While you can't sit in your chair all day and dream (you've got to get up and go do something because faith without works is dead), you also can't dismiss the "asking God in faith" part of manifestation—asking in faith reiterates the truth that God is your Source. Now, I know it sounds harsh, but if you think you can get all the desires of your heart by yourself, you're in pride and you're going to be burned out soon enough. Why? Because you're exalting yourself and your own abilities above the knowledge of God and His power. If you want prosperity God's way, God has to be first every step of the way!

You are not your source. Your job is not your source. Your spouse is not your source. Your children are not your source. Your Source is supposed to be *the* Source, God. We mess up when we choose other people or ourselves to be what only God can be in our life. Nobody can fulfill your core needs but God. When we work with Him and not just on our own, we gain so much more peace and joy as we go after our dreams in life. As believers, it's in *Him* that we live, and move, and have our being—it's not in ourselves (Acts 17:28).

We can't fill those empty places on our own. And we sure can't bring glory to the Father by ignoring His principles and trying to do everything on our own. Who is going to get the glory then? Us—and we'll burn out while patting ourselves on the back for doing such a "great job" at getting what we want. Forget that junk!

Give *God* the glory He deserves by keeping yourself in His will, which is His Word—which means listen to Jesus! Your peace of mind is too important and His glory is too important to dismiss. Make God your Source. Give Him His glory!

Is God Really Interested?
Why Did Jesus Come?

Jesus told us that He came so that *we* might *know* the Father (John 17:3). So, we can be confident that everything Jesus preached was so that we might know the Father's heart and mind concerning us—and learn wisdom about how to live right so that we can live well.

Doing things God's way benefits us at a core level. So, if Jesus says, *"And whatsoever ye shall ask in My name, that will I do, that the Father may be glorified in the Son,"* then He means it will benefit you to ask in His name, and it will benefit you to glorify the Father.

God has a desire to hear *your* voice asking in faith—and pleasing God in this way benefits you. If Jesus says to ask, then that means it is important for *you* to hear your *own voice* asking in faith too—it benefits *you.* And if Jesus says to use His *name* when you ask, then it's vitally important that you use it with full knowledge that you are using the most powerful name on earth—because it benefits *you.* Lastly, if Jesus says He will do what you've asked, then it's important for you to believe that He *will*—faith benefits you. It produces the results you want.

You must convince yourself that God can't lie. His Son is also not a liar. Again, Jesus only said what His Father wanted Him to say. This means God wants you to start asking in His Son's name—not fearing or shifting to natural thoughts, but instead *asking* in His Son's name, with the full belief that Jesus will do exactly what He said. When you ask, believe in your heart that He will respond with, *"That* will I do!" Then, get up and go about your way knowing that it's coming to pass.

If God wasn't interested in doing anything for you, John 14:13-14 wouldn't be in the Bible. If God wasn't interested in being glorified in the Son by you getting your answer, John 14:13-14 wouldn't be in the Bible. After all, why would God compel Jesus Christ to teach you to *ask* in His name if He had no intention of doing anything for you?

If you give up on Jesus' command, if you quit asking and using Jesus' name for anything, again, you are literally hindering the Father's *glory*. Don't do that. Give God the glory He is due! Lose the mindset that says it's selfish to ask. *No*, it's obedient to ask. It's God's plan for you to ask. His glory needs to shine through you to this dark world who needs Him. He wants to give you something they can *see*.

Did You Know That Jesus Often Gave People Something They Could See?

I was voted "Most Changed" when I went to my high school reunion. I guess so! I was a devil from hell before I got saved—and everybody who knew me "back when" could *see* the change in my life. I'm not talking about my brown hair turning gray. I'm not talking about the bell-bottoms and ruffled shirts of the '70s I let go of a long time ago. I'm talking about *who* I am as a man since God got a hold of my heart—and I'm talking about what God has done in life and given to me as I followed His principles and gained faith in His love.

People use their eyes to assess a lot more than you might think. Even Jesus said, and I'm paraphrasing, "If you don't believe what I say, then go ahead and just believe Me for the *works'* sake" (see John 14:11). Think about that for a minute. He was talking about the people who were changed in His ministry just as much as He was talking about miracles like walking on the water and raising people from the dead.

Jesus couldn't go to funerals; He'd mess them up. Jesus didn't care if you already paid for the flowers. Those flowers were going to be trampled by a dead guy coming to life once He gave the word! Jesus taught a lot, but He showed a lot too. What are you showing? Who's getting the glory for what you're doing in life, where you're going, who you are affecting for good, and for what God's blessed you with, too?

If works weren't important, Jesus wouldn't have said look at what is happening. Do you think Jesus was bragging when He said to look at His works? Do you think it was all just spiritual work?

Jesus multiplied food—substance! He took a two-piece fish dinner and caused it to multiply and feed five thousand people. John 6:11 says the people were full and had as much as they wanted—they even had leftovers! Twelve baskets of leftovers isn't just meeting a need; it's going beyond it. Turning water into wine at a wedding and having people ask why the best was saved for last isn't just meeting a need; it's going beyond it. Telling Peter to put His nets out for a catch after he'd been fishing all night and performing a miracle that filled up those nets with so much fish that the nets broke isn't just meeting a need; it's going beyond it. Are those spiritual works to you? Well, they came out of the spiritual realm due to Jesus' faith, but no, they were works that people could see.

Have You Noticed How Jesus' Miracles Were Beyond What People Needed?

Jesus gave His mother what she *wanted* for the wedding. Jesus gave the five thousand who followed Him what they *wanted* when they got hungry. Jesus gave Peter what he *wanted* from the fishing trip. The truth is that those people at the wedding could have just drunk that water. Those people who followed Jesus weren't going to die if they missed a meal—they could have fasted and gotten even more spiritual breakthroughs! Instead, Jesus fed them so much that they couldn't eat it all. Peter surely did *not* need all those fish—that haul was way more than Peter could eat on his own, and obviously more than his nets had been used to holding. So what was the point of Jesus nearly sinking his boat with so *much?*

Jesus bent natural law with His faith in order to meet *desires.* His mother's desires, the desires of people who followed after Him, Peter's desires—every miracle was a desire being met. Why? To give God *glory!* To *show* people the love of God in action through various types of works, encompassing the whole of good desires—spiritual, physical, emotional, mental, provisional, etc.

Lives were turned around and simple desires were met, too. People were raised from the dead *and* gold coins were found in the mouth of a fish—both were miracles, and not nearly the same in weight, of course…but still *done* by God. If it's important to you, it's important to God. If you put your faith toward need, you'll get what you need. If you aim higher, toward want, you'll get what you want. The Bible says you have not because you ask not. The bottom line is that faith is required for it all.

So, think about this the next time you worry about wanting to make more money at your job, or to have more in your business—it's the same as Peter wanting more fish in his boat. Don't let some religious person talk you out of the desires that are in your heart, whether they are life-changing or just day-making. Sometimes it's nice to have a little desire met; it just makes your day, and God does that kind of thing for me all the time. He'll do it for you, too, if you expect it, believe it, and put Him first.

God loves you, and you don't have to put your faith toward only one area, whether it is spiritual or physical or financial—you can believe Him in faith for *everything*. Your everything *is* His anything.

Are You Glorifying God in Your Own Life?

Every blessing or miracle or breakthrough you get from God is a "work," like Jesus talked about wanting people to see—and if you *show* it and you *say* something about it, God will be glorified through your life.

Every single person who *hears* about your answered prayer is hearing about a "work" of God. The same is true when they *see* your manifestation. Glory is the end result—not for you, but for God—if you praise Him about it and tell the story. People love stories. That's why Jesus talked in parables so much. You've got a story to tell about how God has helped you, changed you, blessed you, prospered you, healed you—something! Every

> **Every time you tell your story, you're talking about a work God's done in your life, and that means you are bringing glory to God.**

time you tell your story, you're talking about a work God's done in your life, and that means you are bringing glory to God.

It's almost like whatever you "get" from "asking anything in His name" is almost inconsequential in comparison to the glory God gets when you share what He's done for you. Why? Because God wants you to be blessed. He loves you! The same way Jesus wanted the people to be full, God wants you to be full. Overflow blessings are good!

God wants *you* joyful, blessed, and walking out your destiny as a powerful believer in Him. *You* bring glory to Him when you are blessed. Every challenge you overcome is glorifying the God who gave you the power to be victorious. Every blessing you receive from being a giver is glorifying the God who created the system of sowing and reaping. Every single answer to your prayers brings glory to the God who answered. Give God His glory.

So, *what* is coming out of your mouth? What are you *asking*? What are you *saying*? Are you bringing glory to God? Do you even want to bring glory to God? Did you really think it was *all* about you? Spiritually, physically, financially, or whatever—those heart desires, those simple or complicated requests are *all* important to pray about. You can't get answers if you don't ask questions. And you can't give God glory if you decide not to include Him in your life by bringing your prayers and supplications to Him in faith (Philippians 4:6). He wants to be a part of your life so that you can overcome and get what your heart desires in Him—and He wants everyone who sees and hears to know that He'll do the same thing for them.

Why Not Give God the Glory He Is Due?

If *everything* we could ever need or desire for life and godliness is available through Jesus' name, and it all brings God *glory*, then why *not* ask God for what we want, believe God for what we want, receive what we want, and give the Father the glory He is due?

Once you see that the real "end result" of your receiving isn't *just* what you receive—but also the glory *God* gets as a result of your exchange with Christ—you are going to start looking at your needs, desires, and wants in a whole different way. Why? Because it's not about greed, it's about glory.

Jesus linked *our* asking and *His* doing together when He told us that we can bring glory to the Father in our own lives through our own receiving from Christ. When others see what God has done for us and hear our story, we become walking testimonies to God's goodness.

Jesus wanted to bring glory to His Father when He was on the earth, and He *still* wants to bring glory to His Father today. He will come back for His body of believers one day—we will see Him face to face. Until then, we do our part by being witnesses for Him throughout the earth. What do witnesses do? They tell others about Jesus. They tell what He's *done* for them.

So, while you might be focused solely on the "asking" part (and especially concerned about whatever it is you think is "too much to ask"), Jesus is not worried about that at all! Why? Because His focus is on that "bringing glory to God" part. I believe that your life is going to be a walking and talking testimony to what Christ can do with the childlike faith of true believers.

Nothing is impossible with God. Everything is doable. And every single time *you* receive from Christ, *you* bring glory to the Father—right here on earth. Your blessings *are* God's glories! So, why *not* give God glory and ask in Jesus' name?

Understand that the name of Jesus has been given to you. When you got saved, you were marked with a holy mark, and you are now sealed in His love and grace. His name is on you! It's in you! It will work through you, too.

"Christ in you, the hope of Glory" isn't just a phrase; it's a living reality for all believers (Colossians 1:27). And His name isn't just a name; it's a vehicle of His anointing. Never forget that His name carries His anointing. The Holy Spirit is residing *in* us. Let that sink in. It's going to bless you!

Why Not Ask for What's in Your Heart?

This is so much more than just getting *stuff*. This is about glorifying the Father—and not just some of the time, but *all* of the time. Jesus said that He came that we might *know* the Father. Jesus wanted the world to know that His Father is worthy of glory. He wants us to know that God is good! He is generous, powerful, and able to do "whatsoever" we ask in His

Son's name. Every impossibility that manifests through faith in Christ brings glory to God and shines a light in this dark world.

Do you realize how important it is to *glorify* the Father? Do you realize how important it is, then, to *ask* in Jesus' name for those things deep in your heart? Do you realize how important it is to see the spiritual, physical, and financial desires of your heart come to pass?

"Whatsoever" you desire in your heart is important! Who do you think put those desires there in the first place? If you are afraid to ask for what you want, how much joy do you think avoiding yourself will bring you in the end? Better yet, how much glory do you think you will rob from God if you refuse to honor and ask for the good desires He has placed within you?!

What God put in your heart calls to you because it's meant to. You can ignore it, but you will lose joy—because joy lifts when disobedience remains. Following Christ's teachings brings joy. It brings joy way before you ever get anything that could be lumped into the word "stuff." Faith itself brings peace and joy. Everything you receive in the end is the "cherry on top" of having such a trusting and open relationship with Christ.

So, if you are not obeying Christ's urging to "ask," you really are robbing yourself of more than just "stuff," or inner wants being met—you are robbing yourself of the pure goodness of trust and childlike faith in God. So why *not* ask God for what's on your heart? Don't let fear steal your blessings!

Give God His glory. *Ask* in His Son's name and have faith that it will come to pass, and then praise Him every chance you get. Tell your story. Share your miracle. Don't hide your light at any stage of your growth, but by all means, when you receive, tell somebody. It'll bless you and encourage them—and what will God get in the process? *Glory!*

CHAPTER FIVE

What About Asking "Amiss"—What About Asking for What's Not Right in God's Sight?

*"From whence come wars and fightings among you? come they not hence, even of your lusts that war in your members? Ye lust, and **have not**: ye kill, and desire to have, and **cannot obtain**: ye fight and war, yet **ye have not, because ye ask not**. Ye ask, and receive not, because ye ask amiss, that ye may **consume it upon your lusts**. Ye adulterers and adulteresses, know ye not that the friendship of the world is enmity with God? whosoever therefore will be a friend of the world is the enemy of God. Do ye think that the scripture saith in vain, The spirit that dwelleth in us lusteth to envy? But He giveth more grace. Wherefore He saith, God resisteth the proud, but giveth grace unto the humble. Submit yourselves therefore to God. Resist the devil, and he will flee from you."*

James 4:1-7

Asking "amiss" is often used out of context to explain why believers can't have what they desire from God. It's a false narrative that totally disregards where the verse is situated in the Bible.

Read James 3 and you'll see that it is all about the tongue and how it can stir up trouble for you if you let it run wild. That chapter mentions how you can praise God one minute and curse somebody the next with the same mouth—and if you've ever been in traffic after getting out of a powerful church service and got really aggravated by somebody who just pulled out in front of you…well, you probably experienced James 3:10 firsthand. I know I have!

I've gotten out of a power-punching, Holy Ghost revival and gotten so ticked off ten minutes after leaving church that it seemed like Tabasco sauce was pumping in my veins. I used to get so angry at so many things—and traffic set me off easier than just about anything. *"The spirit is willing, but the flesh is weak"* is in the Bible for a reason (Matthew 26:41)! Like the rest of the Word, it's true that sometimes your flesh gets the best of you and you've got to repent afterward for acting like a fool.

Asking "amiss" is taught in James 4—and contrary to popular teaching, it doesn't have anything to do with God's unwillingness to give us our good desires when we ask for them in prayer. If you want a new home, a new car, a new job, or whatever, you aren't asking "amiss" because that has nothing to do with the passage.

What Is Asking "Amiss" Really About?

The asking "amiss" topic in this chapter has everything to do with a lustful desire to make *war*, a lustful desire to *fight* with others, and the inner war of lust in dealing with *sexual* desire that goes outside of God's will. We know this because it says so!

Go read James 3 and 4 and see for yourself. They are short, and they show you how what you *say* matters and how God will not be partner to the wrongful lusts of the flesh that draw you into sin—things such as verbally fighting, making real war with people, fighting others all the time, and committing adultery.

James 3 gives us a warning about words—it shows us that we do better in life if we aim for *"wisdom that is from above."* It's God's wisdom working in us that is *"first pure, then peaceable, gentle, and easy to be intreated, full of mercy and good fruits, without partiality, and without hypocrisy"* (James 3:17). The last verse of that chapter talks about *peace* and why if we are the righteous, then our fruit ought to be about making peace. It doesn't encourage us to "keep the peace"—it encourages us to *"make peace"* (James 3:18).

I'd say that the first two you need to make peace between are God and yourself. Asking "amiss" only happens when you don't consult God in the first place, or if you don't know who you are in Christ, or if you blow it and pray while you're still in the flesh.

Do You Think God Will Bless What's Wrong in His Sight?

I've found that there are more people who are worried about asking God for anything than there are people who will ask Him for wrong stuff. But apparently there are those people out there, so God had to teach us in James that we can't get Him to do something for us that is obviously wrong. If it's something sinful that you want, you can't expect God to give you what you want.

God won't endorse sin, no matter how much He loves you. So don't even bother to ask Him to sanction your sin. He won't because God is holy. For instance, if what your heart desires is to kill someone who did you wrong, you can't be upset if God doesn't hand them over to you. If what your heart desires is to sleep with somebody else's spouse, do you really think you can ask for that in prayer? If you want another man's wife or another wife's man, God is never going to say, "Oh, absolutely, I'll do that for you!" No indeed!

You can't ask God to condone what's obviously wrong in His sight. That's why you should search your heart for "why" you want whatever it is you want in the first place. It's so that you know your desires are coming out of a good place—a place of purity and not of lustful desires that are sinful in God's sight.

There is nothing sinful about a full pantry, a thriving business, or a new car that doesn't leave you stranded on the road somewhere. There's nothing sinful about wanting to give your children great opportunities in life. There is nothing sinful about wanting new furniture, more property, more animals if you're into that, or a brand-new home for your family.

I'll use the home as an example here. Jesus was a carpenter on earth, and He said when He left for Heaven that He was going to prepare a place for you. So if He wants you living nice up there in Heaven, and His actual job before going into the ministry was making places to live down here, then how can praying and asking Him for a new home for your family be sinful?

Dream big! Let your good desires come up. Let God show you how to expand the dream or vision even more by using your imagination so that you get even better than what you were aiming for in the first place. He is glorified in each good desire that is manifested and fulfilled in your life.

If Your Desire Isn't Good, Can It Really Be from God?

Ask yourself how you can share what you're given—how will each fulfilled desire bless others in your family, your circle of friends, and of course, beyond that too, if it applies. How can your blessings bless others? How much more will you be able to give when you've been given more? How many more people will you be able to support in preaching the Gospel? How can you expand your success to affect the world for good in some way?

You don't ask amiss by asking big—you ask amiss by asking with *sin* on the mind. Yes, sin exists. It wouldn't be in the Bible if it didn't, and you wouldn't be told to ask for forgiveness if you didn't sometimes need it. When it comes to sin, you sure don't need God's help to do it. The devil will make sure you have every opportunity to ignore God and fulfill the lusts of your flesh—just don't take the opportunity. (See Galatians 5.)

Learn from James 3 and realize that it's your own *mouth* that is going to draw you down one path or another—so let the wisdom of God come out more than the wisdom of men. Learn from James 4 and realize that God doesn't grant requests that are rooted in violent or sexual lusts—and that the only way out of that mindset is through submission to God and resisting the devil, which you can do if you will humble yourself before your Creator.

Those chapters show us that speaking evil of others, judging others, judging the law of God, and thinking your earthly life will never end are all foolish ways to spend your time—and asking amiss will naturally happen if your focus is on all that junk. Your focus should be on the good life God wants for you and for everyone in the world. Those kinds of actions come from a heart that isn't focused on God, and consequently they bring no glory to God. They bring no good things to you either. So why would you want to go down that road?

Don't let the devil trap you. *"Submit yourselves therefore to God. Resist the devil, and he will flee from you"* (James 4:7). Humble yourself before God knowing He *wants* to bless you with good things—but you've got to *want* good things, and you've got to *ask* for good things!

Do You Know That the Holy Spirit Is Also a Corrector?

I admit, I've gotten so frustrated by some people who've tried to hurt me or delay projects I want to do that I've been guilty of just being emotional and asking God to take them *out*—like that *Godfather* movie, I want to "get some responsible people" and make the problems go away. That's a joke, but most of us have been there at one point or another when we're so frustrated and can't see a way out. Jesus sent the Holy Spirit to help us with this kind of junk!

So, I know that if you're human like me, you've gotten into the flesh at some point or another since you accepted Jesus as your Savior. And who knows? Maybe you've even asked God for things purely out of the flesh. Maybe you've gotten confused and asked Him for what you know isn't good at all. You can *only* do that when you're in the flesh. If you read the Word regularly, meditate on the love and goodness of God regularly, and make a commitment to talk to God in prayer regularly, you are going to stay sensitive to the Holy Spirit— and that is the key!

When you are sensitive to the Holy Spirit, you will know immediately when you pray for something that is "wrong" for you. I'm not talking about old, guilty religious ideas; I mean flesh-driven requests that bring nothing good into your life. Oh, the Holy Spirit will tap you on the inside and let you know!

That's what I love about the Holy Spirit living inside of us—He is not only a Comforter, but He is also a Corrector! When your spirit is energized with the Holy Spirit, your spirit will send a flag up in your mind if you step out of line. Think of it like this: If you ask something out of pure flesh, your spirit will send a directive to your soul (mind/will/emotions) saying, "That was not right" or "That was not asked in the right way."

The Holy Spirit *will* correct you if you are sensitive. So don't fear asking for what you want. Don't fear the Holy Spirit—*trust* the Holy Spirit. I often call this being "God-inside-minded," and I consider it a form of protection. The Lord will save us from our own destruction if we listen to His promptings. It's no good to get what you want if it's going to destroy you in some way. The Holy Spirit will look out for us if we listen to His correction and take comfort in His wisdom.

So, after all this…are you worried about asking amiss? I sure hope not! Trust the God who trusts in *you*. Trust yourself. If you are a believer and the Holy Spirit dwells in you, you have a built-in divine Corrector who will help you be able to dream big, pray honestly, and ask for what you desire—without fear of going wrong.

Don't let religious people put fear into you about your ability to know the promptings of the Holy Spirit. Don't let them put fear into you about obeying Jesus and asking for things in His name—whether they are spiritual, physical, financial, or whatever! You have the mind of Christ and know all things because of the Holy Spirit within you. This is why it's important to renew your mind to the Word and build your faith with the Word. The Holy Spirit within you will guide you, comfort you, and correct you when you need it—so all you have to do is draw close to Him, be sensitive to Him, and obey the

> **If you are a believer and the Holy Spirit dwells in you, you have a built-in divine Corrector who will help you be able to dream big, pray honestly, and ask for what you desire—without fear of going wrong.**

Word. *Ask* what you will in the name of Jesus and *know* that it will be done for you!

Can You Believe and Do What Jesus Said?

I know I'm stretching your mind and your faith, but can you start believing and doing what Jesus said instead of just relying on someone else's experience? *Yes*, you can. You can start today. If you've neglected this, you can recommit to doing what you know to do. You can start living as God meant for you to live.

I don't care what worked or didn't work for somebody else. What did Jesus say? Who is living inside of you? Whose name do you carry and use? Who has the authority? Who has the final say? Whose report will you believe? Whose report are you going to obey—the world's or the Word's?

I don't know about you, but I want to bring glory to God by believing in faith for everything He has for me and my ministry—and I'm praying and believing for you to have everything God has in store for your life, too. As believers, we're in this together. We're family—God's big family—and we need to support one another by praying for each other.

Instead of being worried about asking amiss just because you want a nice life or a good result, remember the real takeaway from those chapters. Let there be no envy or strife among us who are in God's family. There's enough trouble in the world without believers creating more of it amongst ourselves! I hate strife—and it all starts with one little thing: a flapping tongue.

God's wisdom is critical, good words are important, and peace is God's way—and His peace is something we must *make*. We make it within ourselves first. Any outer conflict is a result of inner conflict in some way. We can't change others, but we can endeavor to make peace.

We make peace inside ourselves when we ask forgiveness from God, if we should go astray, and let the blood of Jesus cleanse us of all unrighteousness. We make peace inside ourselves when we read and meditate on the Word to renew our mind to what is true. We make peace within ourselves when we humble ourselves before God and allow His Holy Spirit to create in us a clean heart and renew a right spirit within us (Psalm 51:10)—so that we can go out and make peace with others.

Let God's wisdom flow in us instead of earthly wisdom. May we bridle our tongue so that we make peace wherever we go. Let us never desire what is not good for us or others. Let us lean on the Holy Spirit in all things. Let good words be on our lips. Let us bring *glory* to God in everything we ask, everything we receive, and everything we do. May our divine family be known for goodness, honor, riches, and great love. Nothing is impossible with God, and that means nothing is impossible for us!

If you somehow mess up with the asking part and somehow do it "amiss," trust that Christ will fix things by prompting your spirit and imparting wisdom to you. Trust that Christ will always bring you right back to a place of love, encouragement, and power. Know that He will always urge you to have childlike faith in Him and glorify God in your life.

CHAPTER SIX

Why Not Let Go and Grow?

I have a granddaughter who has hit a growth spurt, and watching her change reminds me of my own daughter and those years when she was growing so fast that everyone thought she was older than she really was. I love teenagers. A lot of adults gripe about those years because it's true that they kind of lose their mind for while—but they come back. And the challenge for many parents really isn't about the teenager... but about remembering what it felt like to be a teenager.

You have more mercy when you relate personally to how being a certain age feels, so I always say, "Don't forget what it's like to be 13, or to be 16, or any of that...just remember that you were once that same age." You might not be the same type of personality. You probably had a very different life than that teenager has. But the truth is that we all go through some of the same human emotions and challenges. And it's not easy being a teenager. It wasn't easy then, and it isn't easy now. But love can conquer more than hate ever could, and self-disciplining is something you learn.

When you are growing up, you have no control over your own growth. Once, when my wife was in school, they called her house to question her mother—they were worried about her because she hadn't grown taller in nearly three years. She was small for her age as a child. She was a late bloomer. And no amount of Cajun food was going to change that. Her body was doing what her body wanted to do—and until her body was ready, she seemed stunted.

My daughter experienced the opposite in her growth, and now her daughter is doing the same. It seems like my granddaughter is growing two feet every year. She looks two years older than she is right now, and just like my wife when she was young, she can't control her own growth. It's built into the fabric of the body God has given her. She is growing at the rate in which her DNA and God have designed her to grow.

As believers, when we are born again we are not like physical children who grow without any thought or control over our souls—our mind, our will, and our emotions are not fixed to one state and will not automatically get bigger or better. We are malleable like clay, and what we choose to believe, what we choose to let go of believing, or what we choose to say and do will determine how fast we grow—or if we even grow at all.

My daughter says that she can't always see my grand-daughter's growth, and it's not until she sees a picture from a few months ago or a few years back that she really gets just how much she has grown. The same is true with us as believers.

Spiritually speaking, sometimes we, too, have growth spurts, and it's sometimes not until we look back at our lives or our attitudes that we notice just how far we've come. I believe that if you gain a revelation through this book about living by faith and asking in faith, one day, not long from now, you are going to look back and *see* your own growth. You'll be amazed by where God has taken you, what God has done within you, what God has blessed you with, and the huge increase in your own personal faith in His power.

*"And whatsoever ye shall ask in **My** name, **that will I do**, that the Father may be **glorified** in the Son"* provokes a reaction if you really digest the implications. But if you have faith, this can be one of the most growth-surging verses you'll ever read. It challenges us to be childlike in a world that says that being childlike is dangerous. What a lie of the devil!

The devil has been lying since the beginning of our time on this planet. He's even gotten the Church to not only believe his lies but to prop them up in theology to make every blessing something to either be ashamed of or dismissed as evil. Nothing could be further from the truth.

Did You Know That Fear Has Thieving Cousins?

For over 2,000 years, Jesus' teaching in John 14:13 has been right there in the Bible—and for 2,000 years, the Church has chosen *not* to believe Christ's words. In fact, the Church has not only dismissed the teaching altogether, it's actively preached *against* it! Christians preaching against the teachings of Christ—now, that's a crying shame. Why does the Church do this? One word: *fear.*

Fear and all its cousins have stolen the faith that Jesus tried to seed into the heart of early Christianity—faith for not only redemption, but faith for *whatsoever* we need and desire for the life and destiny that God has given each of us. All spiritual needs and desires, all physical needs and desires, all financial needs and desires fall under *whatsoever.* Our "everything" is His "ask anything" in His name.

Fear's cousins are things like self-doubt, shame, guilt, worry, anxiety, and the list goes on and on—and they do nothing but steal your future. All of the cousins are just like fear; they are in direct opposition to the expansive, exciting, and childlike faith Jesus taught us to build by *"hearing, and hearing by the word of God"* (Romans 10:17).

Fear is *always* in direct opposition to faith—and that's not a vague idea, it's just an everyday reality. This is your time to grow and to stretch your faith to the point of not only reading John 14:13, but also accepting and *believing* it.

Do You Avoid "Asking Anything" Out of a Misplaced Sense of Protection?

Many believers don't ask in Jesus' name out of a misplaced sense of protection. They have a troubling fear that they *won't* receive what they ask for. So, to avoid "ruining" Christ's reputation, they decide to just opt out of asking in His name altogether. This is a misplaced sense of protection. Let me give you a word of wisdom here…you don't have to protect the Lord's reputation!

If you avoid "asking anything" in His name out of a misplaced sense of protection, you are really just choosing to replace your faith with fear—and worrying if God's Word is true is just doubt. If you doubt, you can be sure of one thing: You will *not* get what you want.

You have to realize that you don't have the power to protect Jesus' reputation—because the role is one that you were never meant to take. *You* are not God. *You* do not have the ability or the power to protect His Son. God is higher in rank than you. It's not the other way around!

If you want to obey the Lord, ask anything in His name, and see the manifestation of your requests come to pass, then your doubt can't override your faith. Faith must rule. Fear and faith can't both cohabitate in your mind at once—one will always rule in your life. Again, I have to say it: You don't have the power to protect God's reputation in the first place.

When you realize that you've been avoiding asking God for what your heart truly desires, it's easier to let that kind of thinking go. Don't let your mind or the enemy convince you that God is weak and can't do what He said—or that you don't have enough faith to receive.

Because you know that faith can grow, and that it comes by hearing, and hearing the Word, when you feel like your faith is low, it's a signal to get the Word into your ears. Start reading the Word, and do it out loud. Listen to messages based on the Word. Remind yourself of your past victories—of what God has already done for you. And if your mind tries to throw more doubt at you, don't concentrate on pushing the thought out with another thought. Instead, replace doubtful thoughts with faith-filled *words*.

Simple Doubts or Strongholds That Bind—
Did You Know the Word Can Remove Them Both?

Quote the Word to yourself to push out thoughts that aren't good for you. Pick scriptures that apply to your situation and use them for what they are—*double-edged swords of truth* that have the ability to *cut away what needs to go* in your own mind. Read this:

> *For the word of God is quick, and powerful, and sharper than any twoedged sword, piercing even to the dividing asunder of soul and spirit, and of the joints and marrow, and is a discerner of the thoughts and intents of the heart.*

> Hebrews 4:12

Notice, the Word is quick and powerful—this means it works fast and it's effective. It will work quickly and efficiently to help you rid yourself of foolish doubts about God and His power to do anything He says He can do.

Now, it'll never work for you if you don't use it. You can't just read along in church on Sunday, or let it be a fleeting bit of wisdom that goes in one ear and out the other. It's got to get in you, if you want it to come out of you when you need it to work. So, you've got to read the Word and its truths and let it sink into your heart by meditating on it—and most importantly when it comes to conquering thoughts, you've got to *speak* the Word. There is something so powerful when the Word is coming out of your own mouth. Your mind will stop to hear what you are saying, and the doubts will stand down as your faith in the Word you are speaking rises up.

Hebrews 4:12 says that the Word is also piercing to the point of dividing your soul and spirit. Think about that. You see, your spirit man already believes everything God says—your spirit has no doubt because that is the part of you that is most deeply connected to God. Your soul (mind/will/emotions), however, needs to be brought in line with the truth. And that's what happens when you use the Word of God—it pierces through the noise in your own mind and separates those lies from the truth. Your spirit man rises up quickly, then, to conquer the soulish area of your doubts.

I like how it also says that the Word can pierce down to "joints and marrow." This blesses me because it reveals God's power to pinpoint the deepest parts of not only your heart and soul, but it's a reminder that His words can also reach into your physical body and separate what's sick from what's healthy. Every day it seems like we hear how some physical problems start with problems related to our thought life. Doctors warn us about the dangers of stress and how it can trigger and exacerbate all sorts of health issues. But who can avoid the world and go sit on an island somewhere? Even if we all could, we'd still take our mind with us on the trip! And guess what? We'd still be stressed in the mind even if our bodies were doing nothing but laying around burning in the sun.

What happens *to* us is not as important as who is *in* us and whose words we believe and speak to ourselves and over our lives. That is what matters the most for us. God did not create us for continual stress, but gave us Himself so that we might use His peace to overcome the stresses of daily life.

It's the last part of Hebrews 4:12 that I think reveals probably the most important reason we should use the Word to fight our battles—because only the Word can truly *discern* the thoughts and intentions of our hearts. Not our minds—our hearts. That means the things inside our hearts will really drive us, motivate us, and compel us to act in certain ways and make choices for our lives.

What is down deep inside of your heart will be revealed by the quick, powerful, and piercing nature of the Word of God— and not just revealed, but pierced. Have you ever pricked the skin of a balloon and seen how quickly it deflates? When the Word touches what's ailing your heart, it is pierced. And like a balloon, that area is seen for what it is—a big ball of empty air taking up way too much space in your heart. It takes the air out of the junk that has been blown out of proportion in relation to the truth. Sometimes you can believe something for all your life, and all it takes is one bit of truth from God to deflate all that hot air. Sometimes an issue has dug itself in deeply, but the Word can pull up the root so that we can see it and allow it to wither in the presence of truth.

The truth that we know is what sets us free, and there is no greater truth than God's Word. This is why the same verse can affect believers so differently, and why it's been affecting people in varying ways for thousands of years. It's so personal because God is personal, and His Spirit rests on and gives energy to His own words. If you allow the Word of God inside of your heart and let it do its work, it will discern *you*. The Word will pierce the core reasons for any doubt you may have or the core issues that are clogging up your heart, and drain it of its power over you so that you can live free.

"Strongholds" in your life are the areas that you cannot seem to change or let go of with basic human willpower. They act like ropes tied around your heart that keep you from doing what you know to do and keep you bound in a life or a mindset that you really don't want to have. Guess what? Those stronghold ropes can be *pulled* down at a heart level with the power of the Word of God.

You use the Word like a weapon—not on people, but on your own doubts and on any negative spiritual force that is attacking your mind or your life. Remember, it's quick, piercing, and powerful. It's how we do battle. We don't fight people. We don't fight ourselves. We fight whatever is rising up against the knowledge of God in our life.

If the battlefield is in your mind, you need to equip yourself with the weaponry that works to cut away what you don't want hanging around. Read 2 Corinthians 10:3-5 with me and notice how right after it talks about strongholds, it then talks about our thoughts:

> *For though we walk in the flesh, we do not war after the flesh: (For the weapons of our warfare are not carnal, but mighty through God to the pulling down of strong holds;) Casting down imaginations, and every high thing that exalteth itself against the knowledge of God, and bringing into captivity every thought to the obedience of Christ.*

So, you see, it doesn't really matter if it's just a little imagination trying to put itself above the knowledge of God, or if it's a "high thing" in the spirit realm that's attacking you or trying to keep you bound and oppressed in a stronghold of some kind—the Word of God is your weapon.

Are You Willing to Use the Word to "Ask" for What You Want?

You can't "think away" doubt, but you can *speak* away doubt—and you can do it every single time a thought rises up that goes against what the Word says. It isn't hard, but it is a habit you'll want to make if you have something you want from the Lord, a goal you want to accomplish, or even if you just want a more peaceful mind.

Remember that *the Word* lifts the burdens, breaks the yokes, and pulls off the ropes that keep us bound in our heart—it's the weapon of our warfare. And as long as you're going to be thinking and saying something anyway, why not think and say what will draw you closer to God, give you greater peace, and get you what you want (which is a good life, a good outcome, or whatever good thing you have on your heart)?

Personally, I have made it my habit to quote scripture to myself out loud. Why? I say it out loud so that my mind can hear it—if faith is built by hearing, I can't listen to doubt all day and expect to have faith, even if it's just in my own mind.

It's like going to a restaurant and you're really craving a burger. If you don't say you want a hamburger, nobody will bring you what you want. If you just try to think your way to getting a hamburger out of the kitchen, you are going to stay hungry and get resentful that you didn't get that hamburger. So, speak up—say what you want by speaking the Word. Don't serve yourself what you don't want. Don't let yourself be plagued by thoughts that stink up your mind like a rotten plate of garbage. Would you sit down and "eat" what stinks to high heaven? No, in the natural, you wouldn't. So, don't do it with your mind. Serve yourself what is good. Then, use your mouth to speak what's good so that you get what's good—because in reality, that's what you really want.

Sometimes, when my mind tries to go off the rails with thoughts that don't match Philippians 4:8, I say out loud with my mouth, "Those aren't my thoughts! My thoughts are lovely, just, pure! I believe the good report of the Lord, not this junk! Get out!" In other words, I speak so that I can hear my own words—and that forces my mind to stop thinking garbage. It puts something good right where I need it to be—inside my own ears!

You have to speak good things to yourself (not just to yourself, but about yourself), and there is no better foundation for those things than the Word of God. It will swoop in like a double-edged sword, discern your heart and your intentions, and cut away what you do not need to be bouncing around in your mind.

One of the most common things bouncing around is doubt that God won't do what He said—and that sometimes shoots off into thoughts like, "Well, if I ask, I won't get it. I'll ask amiss or I'll say something not right. I don't think I'm good enough or loved enough to get it anyway. Why am I even bothering to ask?!" These kinds of thoughts and others like them will rob you of a good future if you let them—so don't let them. Realize that they are *lies*. The truth is that God will *not* break His Word, and if He sent His Son to teach us about His love, His power, and His desire to give us what we ask, then that is His will for us. He won't break His Word.

Do You Separate Christ from the Supernatural in Your Mind?

It's no coincidence that John 14 begins with Jesus saying this: *"Let not your heart be troubled: ye believe in God, believe also in Me"* (John 14:1). Jesus was about to blow the hat off of the religious status quo of the day. He knew this would be troublesome to the religious crowd. When Jesus said that we should believe in Him just like we believe in God, the Father, He was establishing His divinity—and His supernatural power over men and all of Creation.

Jesus presented Himself as the revealer of God to mankind. Why? Because Jesus wanted His followers to know that He was just as capable and faithful as God, the Father. In other words, He had the power to *do anything*—and that's why He could, with all confidence, teach His followers to stretch their faith and "ask anything" in His name.

Wouldn't you say that it is pointless to ask someone to do something they don't have the power or authority to do? Well, Jesus has all the power and all the authority to do anything. That means He's just as worthy of your faith as the Father. This was a revelation at that time—Jesus was revealing Himself as God, as the one capable of doing *anything*. I can't reiterate that enough.

You see, a Christ devoid of the supernatural is *not* the Christ whom the Gospels invite us to believe. Yet this is exactly what many in the Church want. It's comfortable to remain in the natural way of thinking and believing—but Christianity is really rooted in the supernatural. You cannot separate Jesus from the supernatural because Jesus Himself was and always will be supernatural. God coming down in the flesh isn't natural! Water being made into wine isn't natural. Lepers healed on the spot isn't natural. Food multiplying when you pray over it to feed multitudes isn't natural. Jesus did supernatural things all the time. He hasn't changed now that He's in Heaven. He's the same yesterday, today, and forever—which means yesterday, today, and forever He is *not* devoid of the supernatural.

One of my favorite verses I use to remind myself about God's unwillingness to go back on His Word is found in Psalm 89:34. Here God says, *"My covenant will I not break, nor alter the thing that is gone out of My lips."* Covenant is another word for "promise," and I use this one a lot when I'm believing for something. After I ask God for what I want in Jesus' name, and in faith, I back up my original request with the Word every day—I call in my request with the words of my mouth. This verse is one that I use regularly. I quote it all the time.

In fact, I like Psalm 89:34 so much that I had a huge plaque made with this verse and hung it on the front of my church right under the steeple! Every time the devil or my mind tries to lie to me that something's not working or too much time has passed and I still haven't received what I'm believing for, it reminds me that God didn't mince words in Psalm 89:34— that He meant it when He said, *"My covenant will I not break, nor alter the thing that is gone out of My lips."*

If you are tempted with fearful thoughts about what God can and will do, quote this verse like I do—and do it every time your mind tries to lie to you about God. It will remind you that God is supernatural and He will fulfill His Word, and that His Son will do the very same thing. They are One.

God and Christ are in unison. What Jesus teaches, God agrees with and backs! This means God is willing and He wants us to obey His Son and ask anything in His name. This is something we can do with full confidence because *everything* is doable with God, and nothing is or ever will be impossible with Him. We have His promise, we have His Word, and as we have faith and patience, we will receive *all* we are asking for, in Jesus' name. Amen!

Do You Water Down Christ's Teachings Instead of Having Faith?

I will never water down Christ's teaching to ask anything in His name. I'll never define "whatsoever" as only one thing or one area of life. "Whatsoever" means whatsoever, and asking "amiss," as James 4:3 talks about, isn't a worry because I know that Christ lives in me by the power of the Holy Spirit. And as I said, the Holy Spirit is just as much a Corrector as He is a Comforter. That means you and I can trust God with confidence. We can also trust ourselves.

We aren't sinful, greedy, and hate-filled people living by the lusts of our flesh. We are sons and daughters of God living by the Holy Spirit! We are believers who follow the Lord and know His voice and are endeavoring to live the destiny *He* has laid out before us. We are more than conquerors! And if God is for us, who can be against us?

Don't be against yourself. Be for yourself, knowing that Christ is for you, too! Refuse to let fear or anxiety steal this revelation of Christ's teaching from you. It's in the Word for a reason—and the reason is because *you* need it. I need it. The world needs it. God is powerful and our everything is His anything!

When it comes to your own personal walk with God, let this sink in and become a revelation to you. Your spirit, your body, your mind, and your day-to-day life—all your dreams and hopes for the future—must be anchored in the truth that Jesus is *able* to perform His Word to you. And to me, that's as good as it gets! Jesus can do everything that you need and desire. He can help you overcome anything that pops up in life, too. In Him, you have victory over the devil and all His works, which means you have victory over anything that steals, kills, and destroys in your life. Believe it!

You and I are hooked up to God through our blood-bought salvation, so let's start believing in the words of the One who loved us so much that He gave Himself for us as a sacrifice. It is critical to our growth and success in living the life God gave us. God's purpose was always to give *to* us. Jesus' purpose was always to draw us back to the Father and back to the ways of supernatural faith so that we could receive *all* good things from Him—in every area of our lives. Yes, we begin with the spiritual area, but God is concerned about *all* areas of our life, and He *can* do everything we have the guts to ask and believe for in His holy name. Again, our everything is His anything!

Are You Willing to Water Your Heart with the Dew of Faith?

The very idea of God as our Father comes from spiritual revelation—and from that first revelation comes all of Christ's other revelations. God is a good Father. And His Son's teaching to ask anything in His name is just *one* ray of divine truth Christ shared with us. It's a window of truth into God's giving nature when it comes to us. We are highly favored. We are loved. We are God's children, and He wants us to run to Him with open hearts of faith.

As believers, we cannot take Christ in halves—if He only said what His Father told Him to say and only did what His Father told Him to do, then whatever He said should be taken in full. If He said one thing from God, then *all* things He said were from God. Why? Because He was and is God, in the flesh, for us, right here on the earth. Let's appreciate His wisdom by considering that He *is* the Source of *all* wisdom.

When you believe that your everything is His anything, you are showing that you've got absolute, eternal, and infinite intelligence—because only a fool doubts God. Those who have faith in Him are exercising power on their own behalf just by believing God's supernatural truths instead of man's natural thoughts. It's called using the mind of Christ! That's how you *"know all things"*—it's not you, but Christ that liveth in you (1 John 2:20). You share in His wisdom when you have faith in His Word. Isn't that amazing!?

The very root of your heart is watered with the dew of faith. Just like dew springs from the earth, faith must spring from your heart. Faith refreshes the mind. It uplifts the soul. It changes things because it shifts energy in the spiritual world, and that translates into the natural world. Faith draws the energy that is in God, as well as the spark of His divine energy that resides in you. That's how miracles happen. That's how manifestations of His presence happen. Our faith is so much more powerful than some give it credit for. It's not just words—it's from the heart, and when it lines up with the mouth, watch out! Receiving begins to take place.

As I grow, I realize more and more that every teaching from Jesus is simply Him showing us the way that works for us as human beings—for ourselves, our families, and for the world around us, too. Jesus lived on earth, and He was here for us. He could have stayed in Heaven. He didn't. Jesus taught the secrets of God, and He did that for us. He could have remained silent, but again, He didn't! Christ spoke on our behalf, and through His Word He shows His righteous ways. Everything He did was for us. That's how much He loves and cares for mankind—that includes you and it includes me, too.

When you ask in His name, you will ask the right way. Settle that in your mind. Remind yourself that you are loveable to God and to Christ—see yourself as loved and worthy of everything God has said you can do or have. It becomes easy to trust yourself with "asking" when you know that you are God's beloved. Work on that if it continually comes up as a worry. Let your faith in God's love and truth rise up to cast out the doubt. Remind yourself again that you are God-inside-minded and you don't have to worry because the Lord will always steer you right in all things!

Do You Realize the Breath of God Is Pulsing in You?

All of humanity is lifted into unity and divinity by Christ's revelations. His teachings don't just create goodness and life—

they also inject the hearts of men with an understanding of the unity of mankind and the knowledge that we all share in His divinity. Each of us has the breath of God pulsing in our bodies. This miracle is called life! Without His breath into mankind, none of us would be anything more than dust from the earth. We are *not* just dust. We are speaking spirits who have souls, and we are just housed in this mortal body. Think about the power of the breath of God inside of you right now. Your spirit is powerful.

Christ calls us His bride—we are bound like husband and wife together in the unity of divine love. That is the basis of our faith. Love is the reason God sent His Son. Love is the reason His Son taught us truth. Love is the reason why He wants us to have faith and ask anything in His name. When we have faith in His Word, we are really having faith in His great love for us.

So, if you believe in God, believe also in *all* the teachings of Jesus—and once you know what you want, what your true desire is, then ask for it knowing that God loves you, and like any good Father your growth is important to Him.

Do You See Struggles or God's Word as "Teaching You Something"?

God wants us to know that anything is possible with Him—so do not throw out the words of Jesus just because they seem "impossible." That's the whole point! Do you realize the magnitude of glory that God gets when we ask anything in His name and receive it? Don't let any religious person lie to you and tell you that you should never ask God for your heart's desires.

God isn't a small thinker, and His Son isn't either—why would you ever think God wants you to think small? Why choose limitation? Why choose stunted growth? If Jesus is any example, and *He is the example,* Jesus shows us that God isn't bound by natural law, and He can do anything a person of faith believes Him for. God isn't scared that His kids are going to break Him—He is the God of more than enough. He is limitless and loves to see His children crack off the shackles of doubt and simply believe. It takes faith to grow. Doubt just shrinks us from the inside.

Obey the Word without fear and ask, like Jesus taught. See it as part of your growth to believe by faith that you will receive, like Jesus taught. If you see doubting God's Word as some kind of misguided attempt at growth as a person, then you need to know that mindset is wrong. You must begin to see that *faith* is what helps you to grow as a believer. If you see struggles in life as the only thing that is "teaching you something," you need to turn that mindset around so that you understand that it's *God's Word* that will give you the wisdom you need in life. Don't look at the world's ways and think, *That's just the way it is*—as if God has to work within the confines of that! Turn your mindset around and start seeing *God's* ways as the real way things are meant to happen on the earth, and do happen on earth, if we apply His heavenly principles.

Doubting doesn't make you smarter; it makes you spiritually dumber! God wants to use your growth, your testimony, and your blessings—spiritually, physically, financially, or in any other way—to bring glory to His name and draw more people to His wonderful love.

What Will You Look Back and See at the End of Your Life?

Time only marches forward. Imagine meeting God in Heaven after an entire lifetime here on earth. Imagine looking back on your life. You will see how you've been connected to others and how they have been connected to you. You will look back on your life and answer for your choices, of course—but don't let that get you down if up until now you've made some poor ones. The mercy of God is forever, and His grace is unfathomable. Besides, only God and you know where you started in this life.

Like children, all of us are on a learning curve. We aren't called "God's adults" for a reason! He calls us His children. So, we are learning, growing, and dealing with where we are and what's before us—but we are moving forward in time every day. Will we overcome challenges? Yes. Will we sometimes stumble? Of course. Will we fall? Sometimes, of course. Will we rise up and go again? *Yes!* When babies are learning to walk, all of them take a few hits and fall while trying to walk—but one day, they don't even think about walking. They just walk. And then, before you know it, they start running. They play, laugh, and learn as they go. How do they learn? By hearing and doing, and hearing and doing, again and again!

As believers, we don't just grow challenge by challenge like those who don't know God or listen to Him. Our greatest growth is not pitfall to pitfall and ditch to ditch. Our greatest growth is Word by Word! When our recreated spirit is ignited with faith in the Word, and when we walk in that truth, we grow spiritually. Out of spiritual growth, we make life choices that propel us in the direction of what God has put on our heart—for ourselves, our families, our communities, and our world. The fulfilment that comes from following God's will for our lives just can't compare to anything else—it's what we were all meant to do because it's inside of us to be who we were always created to be.

One day, you will look back on your life—and I believe by faith that you will be proud of what you became, what you did with what you were given, and who you affected in the process of living your life God's way. Imagine looking back and not even remembering where you fell! Imagine looking back and remembering how good it felt to *run* in the direction of your dreams, your visions, and the God-given desires of your heart. Imagine looking back on all the good points and the way God helped you overcome and navigate all the challenges. Imagine ending your time on earth. Will your eyes be cast *down* in regret or *up* in praise to God?

Your Savior loved you so much that He came to not only redeem you but to give you words of *life*—that means words to live by—so that you can fulfill your destiny and reach your destination. The

> **Your personal growth is always dependent on the choices you make to grow—you can't choose where you started, but you can choose where you'll end up.**

joy of the Lord is your strength. His Word is your guide. Your personal growth is always dependent on the choices *you* make to grow—you can't choose where you started, but you can choose where you'll end up.

Will you grow or stagnate? Will you shoot up in faith or stall in fear? Will you wake up tomorrow with a smile, no matter what's going on? Will you dread the day or choose to say, "This is the day the Lord has made, and I will rejoice and be glad in it"? Will you choose to ignore the shifting time and just plod along as if today doesn't matter, or will you choose to have faith and take the day as an opportunity to run your race well? Whose report will you believe—the world's or the Lord's? What choices will you make—to believe for God's best and see His goodness all around you or just expect the worst and complain along with the rest of those who are stuck?

You are never stuck if you've got faith—because only fear keeps you locked in the place called "stuck"! There are no limits in God. Your life here moves forward, but if you're breathing right now you've got something you are meant to experience, to do, and to pass on to someone else. Never forget that your life is valuable, and you will be held accountable for it one day. So, why not charge forward since you're moving forward anyway? Why not give God glory? Why not give Him praise? Why not do what He said and live with faith?

Your everything is His anything. His heart is open to you— let your heart be open to Him and start seeing your spiritual growth as something that you can control. It's not good to end up cynical and filled only with worldly wisdom at the end of your life. There is no joy in that except in the illusion of thinking you know it all, which is a lie because nobody knows it all except God. As people, we learn, grow, and adapt according to what we experience and choose to think, believe, and do.

Don't let the Word be vague to you—something you just repeat in church but don't use every day in life. Don't ignore your own potential by ignoring what it takes to have faith every day. Make the Word personal and realize that God gave you this life in order to experience it and to grow—and not just grow a little, but grow a lot! You grow day by day, if you choose to. So, choose to!

Do You Realize That You Were Created to Grow Big?

All the little changes of your routine, all the choices to speak the Word over yourself to grow, and all the choices to believe in God's love for you are worth it. Everything you do to grow in God is worth the effort because *you* are worth the effort. There is no joy in looking back on a life filled with "shoulda-coulda-woulda" regrets—and you can love God all your life and still have those! How many believers spend a lot of time in church but do not apply the Word to their everyday lives? Don't be one of those who say one thing but do another.

Nobody ever got to Heaven and thought, *Wow, I should have sat around more and done nothing. I should have had less joy and peace. I should have never given love or lived with joy. I shouldn't have grown as much. I should have helped fewer people. I should have given less of myself. I wish I'd never taken the opportunities God gave me. If I had it to do all over again, I sure would have lived lower, worse, and enjoyed myself and other people a whole lot less.* It's funny sounding because it's ridiculous. Nobody ever said any of that!

God put you here to do something not only for yourself, but also the world—did you think your life was just for you? You affect others. You can't even help it. You're a part of God's family, and everyone in the family matters.

By God's design, we are created to grow, to expand, and become much, much bigger than when we arrived on the scene. Spiritually, physically, financially, and in every other good area, we are designed by God to grow…and grow well! Give yourself a boost by looking at today as an opportunity.

Do you have a goal, a dream, a vision, or a desire? Do you just have breath in your body right now? If you have any of those, take the opportunity to have faith in God and in yourself! Today, you are going to grow—and nobody may notice for a while; you might not even notice. Who cares! Growth is happening whether you can see it yet or not. You are going to get "there" wherever there is for you.

Like a teenager who is growing like a weed, if you listen to Christ's words and have faith as you apply what you learn, you won't be able to help but shoot *up!* Day by day and faith to faith, you'll grow. You'll reach your potential. And I pray that you'll look back one day in awe and pure wonder at just how "big" you've become compared to how you started…and just how far God has taken you as you followed after Him. Life is a blessing!

CHAPTER SEVEN

Why Not Give God What He Wishes?

"Beloved, I wish above all things that thou mayest prosper and be in health, even as thy soul prospereth."

3 John 2

"Beloved"—means you are loved. "I wish"—means this is something I sincerely hope for you. "Above all things"— means there is no "thing" I wish more for you than these things. "That thou mayest prosper and be in health"—means I want you to have a very abundant life and a healthy life. "Even as thy soul prospereth"—means I want you to know that your prosperity or health are directly connected to the prosperity of your soul, which is your mind, your will, and your emotions.

I call this verse God's favorite wish for us, the Church— and I know that these words were originally written by the apostle John to his friend, Gaius. I also know that 2 Timothy 3:16 says this, which changes the direction of John's words: *"All scripture is given by inspiration of God, and is profitable for doctrine, for reproof, for correction, for instruction in righteousness."*

So, who is John really writing to? In actuality, while the apostle John may have thought he was just writing to his friend

Gaius, he was really getting these words through "inspiration of God" and that means John was writing scripture to *all* believers. That includes you and me! And like all of the scripture, these words are profitable for us. They are good for our doctrine and help us to know the truth. They correct our wrong ideas about God and give us solid instruction in righteousness.

You could study 3 John 2 and come up with a great theological and critical analysis, but the bottom line is simple: God wants *you* to prosper and be in health. If you are sick, He wants to heal you and then help you to maintain a state of wholeness. Lack is not His wish for you. Abundance is His wish for you.

Why won't we give God what He wishes? God is waiting for us to ask for what is on our heart so that He can be glorified by bringing it to pass. He says, *"Beloved, I wish above all things that thou mayest prosper and be in health, even as thy soul prospereth."* This verse is for us, but a lot of believers don't want to believe it.

The world is filled with people who think Christian prosperity is evil, although the Bible makes it clear that God Himself is not one of those "people." The world is also filled with misguided people who think God puts sickness on people to "teach them something," although there's nowhere in the Bible where Jesus put sickness on anyone. He did the opposite. So, apparently God is not in league with that train of thought regarding health either.

How can we get good things in life from a God we don't believe is good in the first place? Prosperity and health are powerfully linked to the state of your *soul*—which is your mind, will, and emotions. Your perception of things creates your state of mind, which changes how you speak and what you do every day. Our heart and mind must be on the same page.

Is Your Soul Prospering?

Prosperity isn't a dirty word—it's God's wish for you. Health isn't a roll-of-the-dice kind of thing—it's God's wish for you. Your soul has a tie to both of those two things that can help you or harm you, depending on what you allow to rule and reign in your soul.

There are unprosperous souls everywhere you look— lacking what they need to prosper in life and be healthy in their body. There are plenty of people who worry themselves to an early grave. There are plenty of hotheads whose hearts and veins give out before they should. There are just as many despondent people whose unhealed hearts keep them living in a cycle of sadness that steals the "life" out of their everyday living. This is not God's will for us—and it's one reason He sent His Word and His Son. It's the reason I'm a preacher too! It's the reason you share your faith with others. It's the reason we all let our light shine. We instinctively know that God can help the world, if the world will only listen.

What about believers who know God? Do we automatically become prosperous in our soul because we have been saved? No. Our soul is our mind, will, and emotions—and from the moment we get saved, we begin to grow in the knowledge of God and the wisdom of His Word. Our soul is freed more and more as we allow the Lord and His Word to change the way we think with our mind, which then changes our will and our emotions. We have the ability to change our emotional state by going to the Lord in prayer, by reading and speaking His Word over ourselves, and by going out into the world and doing the works of God.

To prosper and be in health, even as our soul prospers, indicates that the soul has the potential for upward mobility—and from that internal state, the outward circumstances of our finances and bodily health change for the better. As most of us who know the Lord understand, there is great healing in the presence of God, and His healing affects our mind, will, and emotions.

If you want your soul to prosper, you need to be open and sensitive to the Holy Spirit. Do not close up your heart and think you can heal and get truly prosperous on your own. You might make headway and even become rich, but if your soul isn't prospering, you won't keep your health and you won't enjoy your money or your things. In fact, you'll find that in the end, what you wanted wasn't even what you really wanted in the first place! Every "thing" gets old. We enjoy them but we can't put any "thing" ahead of God in our lives and expect good results. That's ridiculous!

The Holy Spirit was sent by Jesus after He rose from the dead. He is a key player in bringing your soul up the ladder of prosperity. We have a Comforter in the Holy Spirit. He leads us to the One who is our Healer and the Lifter of our head. He is with us and in us, as believers, and we have access to His soul-lifting power every single day. Anyone who dares to be healthy can go to Him with brokenness and He will begin to heal and bring wholeness. We can empty ourselves to Him knowing that He will love us, hear us, and accept us for who we are right in the moment—and He won't hold it against us. He can take it!

You can't break the Lord. He is forever strong for you and compassionate at the same time. In fact, He sees beyond where you are. He knows who you are meant to be and He also knows what He can do if you ask Him and apply His Word.

Jesus is moved with compassion for all who feel lost or need healing. He is the Good Shepherd, the Great Physician, and He can handle every soul's need. He's also a Friend when you need it—always there, always ready, and always willing to go the distance with you.

Remember that Jesus knew He was going to raise Lazarus from the dead, and yet He still cried with Martha and Mary when He came to town for the funeral. Why? Because He was moved with compassion for the state of their souls in that moment. Jesus has not changed.

If your soul is sick, the Lord has time for you—He has all the time in the world for you, and all the wisdom you need to heal up. But don't take all the time in the world to go to Him though! What Jesus reveals, you can leave at His feet. You don't have to walk around in soul-lack or soul-sickness and rehash the same junk over and over. Go to Him and dare to let it go. Have faith that He will raise you up from whatever has brought lack and sickness into your mind/will/emotions—that the Lord will help your soul to prosper in the quickest way that it can. After all, you've got a good life ahead of you! And you start living it the moment you acknowledge Him—so it's just more of letting Him in to do the work that only He can really do.

If your heart is broken, the Lord is near to you. His Word says, *"The righteous cry, and the Lord heareth, and delivereth them out of all their troubles. The Lord is nigh unto them that are of a broken heart; and saveth such as be of a contrite spirit. Many are the afflictions of the righteous: but the Lord delivereth him out of them all"* (Psalm 34:17-19).

Acknowledge His presence knowing that the Lord is listening with ears to hear you. Remember Hebrews 13:5: *"...for He hath said, I will never leave thee, nor forsake thee."* That's talking about Jesus promising to never leave or abandon you. So you can count on Jesus being with you right in the moment you call out to Him, in whatever state of mind you may be in at the moment. But no matter how you come, He will not leave you the same way. His love changes you, and His power is in that great love.

If you are willing to allow Him, He will be the Lifter of your head. If you are willing to look up to Him and to His Word, He will set your eyes on things above and not on things below—in other words, He will give you a new and better perspective.

Truth changes the way you look at things, and there is nothing truer than the love Christ has for you. He wants you prospering at a soul level, and He's willing to get in there with you and make it happen! Jesus will fill you with His love and guide you in His Word so that every soul-sick thing is pushed out in His presence and in the light of His truth.

Do You Realize That "Inner Prosperity" Is the Catalyst?

"Inner prosperity" produces outer results—it's the catalyst for prosperity and health, according to 3 John 2, showing us that it's from a prosperous soul that we gain a godly, prosperous life.

As your faith rises, so do your results. You ask, and in time you receive. You apply a principle, and it's not long before it begins turning things around for you. The devil sees and fights, a challenge comes, but because your soul is prospering, your faith rises and you overcome his dumb challenge and receive what you wanted from God anyway...but with a story to tell on top of the blessing! Ha! The devil can't win. You overcome by the blood of the Lamb and the word of your testimony, and that's that—because that's what prosperous-souled people do (Revelation 12:11)!

It all happens *as* your soul prospers—in other words, you don't have to be fully soul-prospering to see results. You just have to ignore the soul-sick words of this world so that God's words can take up those places in your mind. His words come in like a flood and change things! When you hear them, they set you free. Your emotions go somewhere good instead of where they've been going. That helps you have a greater will to do good things for yourself, for your family, for your community... for the world you live in.

Soul-sick ideas, words, and choices are what this world runs on, and do you see the problems that happen as a result? Prosperity is of God. It begins inside. And as we prosper in our soul, it makes its way into our everyday life in the form of bigger opportunities, nicer "things," better experiences, and my favorite—better stories to tell that help others find God's good ways too! There is nothing better than spilling your healthy soul onto others. There's no better feeling than spilling your prosperity everywhere you go.

Don't be afraid to prosper and be in health, even as your soul prospers. It's God's wish for you! Now, when are you going to give God what He wishes? C'mon! It's in the world's best interests for you to be healthy and prosperous—spirit, soul, and body. It's not only good for you and for everyone who crosses your path, but it blesses God in Heaven, too!

The way to start your soul on a journey of prosperity is with the Word of God. We wouldn't be encouraged to "renew our mind" with the Word if we didn't need to have our perspective changed with truth (Romans 12:2). And the scripture verses that we use aren't just dead words on a page but are living and active. The Word is called a "twoedged sword" for a reason—it cuts out those things in you that aren't good or necessary, while at the same time it slices through the atmosphere creating changes in the spirit realm, which begins changing the physical realm. We'll get to more on that in a minute!

The Lord can take you from one place to another in life, but it's always Presence to presence and Word to word. In other words, it's Jesus and you creating something that starts on the inside. His Presence and your presence. His Word and your word. The soul-work isn't as hard as you think, even if you have a lifetime of baggage in there!

Before you know it, the prosperity you build in your soul starts showing up in your everyday life. The time frame seems to get even shorter when you come to the realization that your "everything" really is His "ask anything"—when you grasp that God gets all the glory when you receive from Him. "Things" then become exactly what they've always been—just good things!

Do You Know What All the "Things" in the World Can't Do?

As a young man, I remember getting a lot of money and sadly realizing that things didn't do what I thought they'd do—I was so disappointed they didn't make me happy. If the goal of having things is to fulfill a void in the heart, you'll be disappointed in the end no matter how many things you get.

Some people want prosperity on the outside, but they don't want to touch the unhealthy areas of their soul. That's when "things" have the potential to become something they were never meant to be, which is just a bunch of substitutes for heart issues. God says He will give us all things to enjoy. He didn't say they were supposed to do anything other than bring enjoyment.

When a person's soul isn't healthy, they will replace the enjoyment of a thing with a desperate desire to meet a heart issue—and that thing can never do it. So the thing ends up being a poor-performing replacement for whatever they never got earlier in life. That's why they aren't satisfied for long with whatever "thing" they get. They might enjoy the emotional high for a brief time, but it wears off...and they go looking for one more "thing" just to keep pumping themselves up.

For instance, the person with an unprosperous soul might think buying more things will make them feel like they are "enough" as a person—if they *have* enough, then they must *be* enough. Wrong. God made us enough the moment He created our spirit. The lie of the enemy is that you are "not enough"—let that lie go because with God, you are way *more* than enough! There aren't enough "things" in the world to fill the "not enough" void of a person's heart. Jesus can do that in a moment. The principles of His Word can then teach a person the truth so that they can let go of the old lies about themselves and start having some faith in God.

Other people with unprosperous souls think that if they could only take that long trip to the beach, they'll be able to unload all their stresses and gain real inner peace—as if two weeks out of the year is going to make all the difference in the world. Unless you meet Jesus on that beach, no matter how gorgeous that beach is, you're just going to come home sandier than when you left. You'll be calmer, maybe. You might be burnt. But I guarantee you that no matter how good the vacation is, your life will go right back to status quo when you get home if your soul isn't prospering. You see, a beach trip can be calming and good for your mind in some way, but there is no way it can meet the need for peace at a soul level. In fact, many people think getting away can fix marriages, but common sense tells you that you can fight with your spouse just as much at the beach as you can sitting around the house!

There are so many ways that people whose souls are not prospering try to make "things" give them what only God can give them—but the truth is that you can have *both* the heart issues met and the nice things you want. Stop choosing the lesser one. And don't just choose the greater one. Abundant living is choosing both!

Deal with your heart and you'll enjoy the "things" you want in life so much more. You won't be trying to weigh them down with emotional junk—you won't mistake what things can do for you or confuse getting new things with real fulfilment. You'll be content in your own heart with who you are and *whose* you are, and then you'll just enjoy your blessings for what they really are—which are nice things that God wants you to enjoy. Sweet enjoyable additions to your already prosperous soul!

Do You Know the Inside Out Truth About Change?

The power of the Word of God to change a life is great—but only to the degree that it actually gets off the bookshelf or out of the computer and into your mind and heart. The Word is filled with teachings that, when applied, have the power to change our life from the inside out. That's how you change, you know. It's not outside in. It's inside out! You can't clean a fish before you catch it—God must have your heart before you can really make changes that will stick.

You also don't lose weight from the outside—your body takes it from the inside, and that's why it takes a little while for you to see your good efforts and choices in the mirror. You're just looking at your outside when you're dieting. You might be trying some clothes on or staring at yourself in the mirror, thinking that nothing much is working. But you can't see all the fat and fluids that have been disappearing bit by bit from around your organs. You can't see the pressure to your heart or to your knees that's being alleviated with each ounce lost from the inside of your body.

This world is so cruel about bodies, so judgmental about how you're "supposed" to look—but I promise you that the most important thing is your health, because let's be honest, you're going to get as skinny as you ever could be once your body is dead! Oh, you're going to waste away to skin and bones then. Ha!

I don't care what people think about my body, because it's my body! God didn't give it to them; He gave it to me. Your body is your own, and you only get one. So, I say, enjoy yourself. Enjoy the body God gave you. But take care of it because it's how you're getting around this place! Do you want to live? Do you want be healthy? Don't just think about cutting back on unhealthy junk when it comes to what you put in your mouth—think about reconditioning and feeding your soul.

Your body is a follower. It's your mind that needs to get healthy. It's your emotions that need to get healthy. If you just focus on the body, you'll just yo-yo forever. You must focus on prospering your mind, will, and emotions if you want to prosper in your body. I fought my weight my whole life, and it took me a long time to get to the place of eating anything I want, but just less of it. There are a lot of fads out there. Many work. But nothing will work long-term until your soul prospers in that area.

If you want to make changes, start in your soul—you will start there for every part of you, not just your body. Anytime you are making changes to yourself, any time you want to prosper and be in health, you must see the soulish part of you as a link to the end result that you want. You can't just ask God for prosperity in life if you aren't willing to do what He says and renew your mind—to see that He's already given you an "even as thy soul prospereth" bit of wisdom that you need to use.

Don't delude yourself into thinking that you're somehow going to see your changes outside in the real world before there are changes inside the inner world of *you*. The Holy Spirit is full of peace that calms when you need it and fire that energizes you when you need that, too—it's both a calmer when you need it, and it'll light a fire under your butt when you need that, too!

Are You Listening to the Two Voices That Matter?

It's time to believe God's voice in 3 John 2 is true: *"Beloved, I wish above all things that thou mayest prosper and be in health, even as thy soul prospereth."* It's time to accept the words of Jesus in John 14:13-14 and do it in faith: *"And whatsoever ye shall ask in My name, that will I do, that the Father may be glorified in the Son. If ye shall ask any thing in My name, I will do it."*

I believe God is saying this to us: "Oh, I *wish* you would do that! I wish you would believe Me for more because I want to do more in your life. I wish above *all* things that you prosper and be in health. From your soul to your daily life, I want to see you doing well. I need you to know that I love you, I'm with you, and I want to bless you in every way. Have faith! Ask! You will glorify Me by asking in My Son's name." That's what God's voice sounds like in my heart—

> I believe God is saying this to us: "Oh, I wish you would do that! I wish you would believe Me for more because I want to do more in your life."

God supports His own Word, and He is supportive of me too. He has good intentions, always, when it comes to me. The same is true for you.

Voices. There are a lot of them in this world. There are distractions everywhere you look. If you share your heart, your goals, your dreams, and what you're asking God for, there are bound to be people who have something to say about it. Let me tell you something, the voices that matter aren't always the ones that scream the loudest. Only two matter—God's and yours.

Don't listen to those people who don't believe in you. God believes in you! If you know that and you believe in yourself, too, you won't be waylaid by the other voices in your life that tell you what you *can't* have, what you *can't* do, or what you'll *never* accomplish in life. Who cares if they say you can't? God says you can. Do you say you can? Get "can't" out of your vocabulary. Stop believing in the power of "can't." Don't waste your energy on rehashing what the "can'ts" of life say. Nothing is impossible with God, and if He put something on your heart to ask or do, then you can ask for it and you can do it.

Make the Word personal. Make it the primary voice you hear. Make your voice the secondary one. Why? Because if God's Word is not the primary voice and if you aren't using your voice to re-establish what is true, other voices that you hear will try to dominate your life. And those voices may be flat wrong. The "can'ts" in your life will regurgitate the world's ideas about whatever you *should* be doing or who you *should* be—or what you *shouldn't* ask God for or what you *shouldn't* even desire. Forget those voices! They don't matter.

When God called me into the ministry, I didn't hear one good voice telling me, "I agree with you, Jesse. You're called into the ministry. God is going to use you for good, boy!" No, even my own pastor tried to talk me out of it. Nobody believed in me. I guess it was OK because I didn't really believe in me either! You see, I already knew I wasn't "preacher material." I'm Cajun French. I'm not a typical pastor type of person. I have a serious past that God saved me from. I sometimes get irritated and speak my mind. I don't come from Texas! There were and still are a million reasons why I thought (and everybody else thought) God shouldn't call me into the ministry. Guess what? None of that mattered!

When God says something to you, and you know it, you have to stick with it—even if other people can't see it. If you can't see it, you just have to have faith that *He* is right and He will do what He said He will do. In other words, you just have to obey His voice. It must be the primary voice. Once you do that, you can just say what He says. That's what I did. I said I was a preacher even when I didn't "feel" like I was a preacher—when I thought I wasn't qualified, I repeated what God had told me...that I was "called."

God's word to you is powerful—it'll guide your life to places you never thought you'd go. Don't worry about being "unqualified" if God has told you to do something. Just repeat Him. Say what He says. Take it on faith. Decide that you don't have to know all the details up front—you just have to trust Him, obey Him, and take the opportunities He gives you. It'll be hard to do that if you focus on the naysayers and the "can'ts" in your life. But it will be easy if you just listen to the Holy Spirit and repeat after Him. The voice of the Holy Spirit and

YOUR **EVERYTHING** IS **HIS** **ANYTHING**

your voice are the only voices that matter. Those are the two voices that will get you where you need to be!

All the voices that go against God's Word in this world are wrong, and any voice that rises up to deliberately hurt you isn't flowing in His good spirit—and I don't care if that voice is your mother, your sister, your brother, or like what happened to me…your pastor! I was a talented musician, and when I joined that church they asked me to help with the choir. So I did. I took that sad and miserable sounding bunch of people and turned them into a kicking little choir, man! I had fun. We all worked together and it made the music in the church something worth hearing. People liked me in that church. Looking back now, I can see that maybe it wasn't just the Cajun accent or the broken English I used that caused my pastor to not want to see me preach the Gospel. Sometimes it's just about power—who has it and who doesn't want you to have any of it.

There is a lot of jealousy, envy, and fear about success in the world. Just remind yourself that none of those other voices matter. If they are hate-filled, judgmental, fear-filled, envious, jealous, competitive, or mean-spirited, they aren't what you should allow to get inside your head. Those kinds of voices mean *nothing* in the light of God.

God loves you, has plans for you, and it's His good will to help your soul prosper so that you are prosperous and healthy in life. So, if the "can'ts" start up, don't let their voices cause your soul to wilt. God's grace is sufficient for you, and the only voices that really matter are His and your own—they'll grow you, they'll cause you to bloom, and one day nobody will be able to deny what God has done in you. Say what God says and throw out the rest!

Do You Know That
Confidence and Faith Come as a Pair?

People ask me how I'm so confident about what God will or will not do. Well, I believe that confidence is linked with faith. Just like fear and doubt go hand in hand, faith and confidence show up as a pair. So, I've decided to choose the good pair and enjoy the ride.

You see, you can't even really separate faith and confidence because one is always an expression of the other. So, I don't have to build up my confidence. I just focus on believing God in faith, and out of that belief confidence in Him and my own abilities starts rising, too. The bottom line is that when you choose faith, you are choosing confidence too—in God, in Jesus, and in yourself. In other words, you don't wonder if He's listening! You *know* He hears your every word. You also know that He loves you, life is an adventure of faith, and that you are more than able to live it well and receive from Him— whether it's financial blessings, opportunities, favor, wisdom, or whatever it is that you desire.

And this is the confidence that we have in Him, that, if we ask any thing according to His will, He heareth us: And if we know that He hear us, whatsoever we ask, we know that we have the petitions that we desired of Him.

1 John 5:14-15

It helps to remember that the Spirit of Christ is *in* you—so you can feel good about becoming one with that name. Do you remember the *"Christ in you, the hope of glory"* scripture from Colossians 1:27? Remind yourself of just who lives and moves and has His being in *you*. Christ is not outside of you, so you should never feel uncomfortable using His name. You have His Spirit, you have His Word, and you have His permission to use His name—it's a gift of authority, and one you must take if you want to receive from God.

The more we accept who we are in Christ, the less fear can take hold of our minds. In fact, I believe that when the anointing of Christ is pulsing in us, we fear nothing within or without. The anointing destroys everything that would try to weigh us down. Faith rises, and asking of God becomes as natural as a bird flying in the air—something it's supposed to do!

Again, I believe it was no coincidence that Jesus' first verse in John 14 was, *"Let not your heart be troubled: ye believe in God, believe also in Me."* Jesus knew what He was about to teach on—and He knew all of us would have to firmly accept the fact that we could believe in Him. We could put our faith in Him, just like we put our faith in God.

You've got to be brave to have faith! Bravery, endurance, and victory are not accidental. They are necessities of life. So, what are you going to ask God for? What are you going to ask God about? Open yourself up to God—and keep yourself open. Use the name of Jesus with reverence, authority, and power. It's time to receive.

Are You Willing to Be Brave... and Not Hold Back?

My daughter was never one of those kids who was constantly asking me for something. Even today, I can count on two fingers how many times she's asked me for help. Why? I don't really know, but she had a real problem with receiving for a while. I'd try and bless her and she'd say, "Oh, no, Daddy, I don't need that, I'm fine."

I'd try to give to my daughter, but she could barely take it. It hurt me sometimes to have to teach her over and over how to receive—she assumed receiving was the same thing as "taking," and she didn't want to be a taker in life. I spoke a message years ago called "The Choke Hold," which she inspired. She isn't like that today. She seemed to grasp the nature of a giving parent a lot more once she had a child of her own, but it just goes to show that it doesn't matter what you've heard—unless you accept it and believe it for yourself, you won't experience all God has for you. God is *the Giver*. Get over the mental hurdles in receiving from Him, and you'll not only be a lot more blessed, but you'll give Him a lot more joy, too.

The language of hesitation crops up in some people more than others—they'll hold back when God is ready to pour out blessings on them. They'll literally stop the blessings, on purpose, when they think they don't "need" it or deserve it, or they just don't want to be seen as a taker. God knows who you are. He sees your heart. But you need to see *His*. God is a Giver. When we hold back and don't ask, we rob Him from the joy of doing good things for us—we rob others from the joy of seeing Him as a Giver, too.

Beware of the language of hesitation—realize when you are holding back with God. True bravery of the spirit is what you should be aiming for. Hesitating to use faith doesn't prolong receiving; it stops you from receiving. If anyone should be brave, if anyone should be fearless, and if anyone should be thinking well, talking well, and living well, it should be the body of Christ. If we know God loved us enough to send Jesus, we should know God loves us enough to honor our faith in His Word.

There is a lot of ignorance, superstition, and false narrative surrounding wants and desires, but I've learned to dismiss anything that goes against "asking anything in His name"— because those are the words of Jesus. I've come to believe that anybody who rejects Jesus' teachings is rejecting God's will for their lives and consequently will live far below where they should in life.

It's a tragic error to say that God wants His kids broke, sick, and barely getting by in life. It's a tragic error to dismiss miracles and faith. It's a slap in the face to the God who rained manna from Heaven, quail from the sky, and parted the Red Sea. It's a slap in the face to the One who healed the lepers, raised the dead, and produced food for over 5,000 people with a faith-filled prayer and a two-piece fish dinner.

I don't care how cowardly some people are; when it comes to doing what Jesus said, I've made up my mind to simply believe that God is able and to just do what Jesus said and ask for what's on my own heart. I've made up my mind to get up and walk forward in faith because I *know* that God wants every part of my life healthy and prosperous.

I love 2 Timothy 1:12. There it says, "*...I know whom I have believed....*" It's such a powerful statement, and it inspires me so much because we need to get beyond just believing and into *knowing* in whom we have already believed. So, if being prosperous and healthy in my soul and in my life is what God wishes, then why not give Him that?

God wishes that *you* prosper and be in health, even as your soul prospers—so let's give Him what He wishes! Ask your Father in Heaven for "whatsoever" is in your heart. Work on your soul and don't have a shred of concern about what's "too much to ask for." There is no such thing because "whatsoever" means whatsoever.

I pray that as you grow in understanding about the limitless love and goodness of God, you'll find new bravery of spirit as you pray, and fresh boldness of faith as you bring your requests up to the Lord. I pray that you get a solid "knowing" in your heart that it gives God pleasure to bless you, and that He glories in taking care of you as you move through every stage of life. Make God happy today by giving Him what He wishes!

CHAPTER EIGHT

Why Not Give God Pleasure?

*"Let them shout for joy, and be glad, that favour
my righteous cause: yea, let them say continually,
Let the Lord be magnified, which hath **pleasure** in
the **prosperity** of His servant."*

Psalm 35:27

The word *pleasure* freaks out a lot of Christians. We seem to think that there is some higher value in sorrow and misery as Christians than there is in joy or peace of mind. But read the above verse in Psalms and ask yourself, if God Himself takes pleasure in our prosperity, then why don't we?!

If it makes *God* joyful to give, why are believers so scared to ask? If it gives Him happiness when we are prospering, why does it make us so nervous to aim for success in life? Everywhere I go, I encounter wonderful Christian people who genuinely still think it is wrong to want to be prosperous— even the word *prosperity* makes them flinch.

John 10:10 says that Jesus came to give us life, and life in abundance. He didn't come to earth to tell us what a bunch of low-down and dirty dogs we were. John 3:17 says He didn't condemn anyone, but He came to save everyone. What did

He come to save us from? He came to save us from *everything* that isn't "life and life in abundance"—so that means He came to save us from misery on earth just as much as misery after death.

It's hard to think of two things in life that are more miserable than living in poverty or living in sickness. Both of those steal, kill, and destroy your life in some way or another—and again, we know all stealing, killing, and destroying have their roots in the enemy and his plans to harm mankind (John 10:10).

Jesus went to the cross to redeem us and give us power over the devil and all his works—works that are marked by stealing, killing, and destroying our lives in some way. God gets no pleasure in seeing us robbed of joy or peace. He gets no pleasure in seeing us being killed a little bit more every day by the pressures of lack. No matter what we gain in life, if we lose ourselves gaining it...well, we haven't gained anything of value at all. Suffering and misery aren't God's best; it's the devil's worst!

There is a mentality in the Christian community that suffering and misery are what we should feel proud about—that our endurance alone is what marks us as believers. We're often still being taught, either outright or just by the examples of others, to "succumb" instead of "become."

I don't believe we should ever lay down and just take what the devil hands us. Why should we? Should we just lay back and be content to complain like the rest? That old cliché "misery loves company" sure is clichéd for a reason—but I don't want to be miserable, and I don't feel good inside seeing anybody else that way either.

Do You Think "The Valley" Is Holy or That "Lack" Gives God Pleasure?

If your prosperity brings God pleasure, do you think that your lack can also give Him pleasure? No! God is not double-minded. He does not want to see you living with a mindset of lack any more than He wants to see you living in *any* area of lack.

Psalm 35:27 says, *"Let them shout for joy, and be glad, that favour my righteous cause: yea, let them say continually, Let the Lord be magnified, which hath **pleasure** in the **prosperity** of His servant."* This verse shows us that God has zero problem with prosperity if you are serving Him. Are you serving the Lord? You qualify for godly prosperity.

Do you think that the challenges you face in life are something that God takes *pleasure* in? No! He doesn't take pleasure when you go through things in life. And it doesn't matter if your challenge is marked by a lack of health, a lack of finances, a lack of favor, or a lack of whatever—God gets no pleasure in any form of lack whatsoever in your life. The scripture plainly says that it's *prosperity* that brings God pleasure, *not* lack. I can't say it enough!

Any "valley" or challenge that has the mark of lack on it can't possibly be something God wants you to stay in. It's not His will for your life to remain in any state of lack. "Valleys" in life are not meant to be seen as permanent places for the believer. Still, most Christians don't go *through* the valley (Psalm 23:4)—they stop, pitch a tent, pace around and complain with others…and then, they canonize the place! In other words, instead of doing what they need to do in order to go *through* the challenges, they convince themselves that God must *desire* for them to live there in the lack valley.

God doesn't want what the devil wants! God doesn't take *pleasure* in you staying in a stealing, killing, and soul-destroying place in life. Don't turn what the devil meant for harm into a holy place in your own mind. Don't let some worn-out idea of holiness trick you into thinking that God gets pleasure from your suffering. I don't care how long tradition has told you a lie, it's still a lie—the valley is not holy. God doesn't rubber-stamp the devil's work and call it good, and neither should you!

The valleys in life aren't places we should just lay down in and accept as permanent. No, we resist the devil. We use the Word. We put our faith in God and *speak* to problems like Jesus spoke to the wind and the waves. In other words, we overcome the valley through the blood of the Lamb and the word of our testimony, and we become sharper, stronger, and more confident as we walk through the challenges of life.

We don't "succumb!" We *become*.

Why "Succumb" When You Can "Become"?

I've had many opportunities to fail, I just didn't take any. Why? Because I know that nothing good comes from lying down in a ditch. Nothing good comes from giving up. You can have a moment there, but then talk to God and talk to yourself, and get up! Lift your head, laugh at the devil, and let the Word you've planted in your heart come out your mouth. Sometimes in my life, I've had to say, "A fight you want, devil, a fight you're gonna get!" I've had to "hit it in tongues," pick myself up, shake the dust off, and keep on believing that what God said, He will do—and no challenge in life can take that away from me. I refuse to succumb. There's more for me to do, and there's more for you to do, too.

As believers, we are more than conquers, not less than conquerors. We learn a lot as we go through challenges. We don't just learn what we're made of; we also have faith in what *God* can do. We aren't alone. God is with us. We don't have to succumb. We're meant to *become* people of stronger faith, deeper wisdom, greater compassion, and greater generosity of spirit.

We are often purified in the fiery challenges—if you are never tested, you'll never know what's inside of you. Rising above and letting faith carry us through the fires, the flames, and the valleys of life glorifies God and gives us peace that passes all understanding (Philippians 4:7).

In other words, the fruit of the Spirit within you rises up to the challenge when you allow it to, and it carries you through things that would totally derail and ruin others who only rely on themselves. We rely on our faith in God. It doesn't just insulate us and protect our minds, but it literally turns our situations around. Like they say, you can't have a testimony until you've had a test.

Believing that Jesus said to "ask anything in My name and I'll give it to you" is only believable to you when you accept that

God Himself is generous and abundant—and that there is *no* lack in Him whatsoever. You become a more generous person when you accept the truth that you serve a generous God—Jehovah Jireh, your Provider! This is in *all* areas of your life.

In every challenge and victory, your goal should be to *become* a better giver and receiver of whatever prosperity God puts in your hands—spiritually, physically, financially, or in whatever area God gives you the opportunity. More love! More joy! More peace, longsuffering, gentleness, goodness, faith, meekness, and temperance—this is what we get and what we "become" when we refuse to "succumb" to the more common ways of thinking/being/doing that are in the world's system.

What the devil means for harm, we allow God's Holy Spirit to turn around for good. What could have made us bitter actually makes us more merciful. What could have made us hard actually makes us gentler. We aren't taking the devil's bait and we aren't listening to what the world says because we want a better future—and we know that if we succumb, we can't become who we're meant to be.

So, whatever the challenge, remember that you are passing through! You're not meant to camp out in the low places of the heart and the mind. If you fall, you rise back up. You choose to because, well, what else are you going to do? Anybody can lay down in the muck and complain. But God has given us His Holy Spirit and the wisdom of His Word. This is what helps us to change our perspective to abundance so we can become the kind of believer who "asks anything" in Jesus' name and expects to get it.

The wisdom of the Word and the power of the Holy Spirit working in us helps us to become the kind of believers who decide to choose the better options in life—to choose love, joy, and blessings. We aren't afraid of giving God pleasure, and we aren't afraid of having pleasure in our own lives either. When challenges come, our faith in God rises up, too. Instead of succumbing like the rest of the world, we rise up in faith to become "more than a conqueror." We become gentler people, more patient, and with more of God's goodness, faith, meekness, and self-control filling our lives.

Is the "Driver" of Your Desire Good?

Some of the most joyful and generous believers I've ever met haven't had it easy—but God has taken them through the darkest of times, the hardest of challenges, and raised them up with His Holy Spirit. So even though they "should," by the world's standards, have given up all hope and lost all joy, they are actually beacons of light who show others that it's possible to overcome and live a good life, no matter what. It's like their very lives are saying, "Look! Here's the Way out! Here's the Truth that will set you free! Here's the Life that will pick you up, help you rise up out of those ashes, and make you new again! Let me tell you about my Jesus—and if you don't want to hear it, just look at my life and see what He can do!"

Challenges don't have to break you. Take me for instance. My life was not easy. It's still not always easy. I've told my testimony in other books, so I won't get into it here—but I came out of base poverty, hardship, and abuse. My parents weren't bad people. They just did to me what was done to them.

They were wrong in so many ways, but here I am today, and I'm blessed, joyful, and still full of energy for the calling God has put on my life.

I came from nothing. I was told I'd be nothing. I was called stupid and that I'd never amount to anything—things nobody should ever say to anybody, let alone a kid. Was what they said about me true? No, but I heard it enough and believed it enough to let the fire rise up in me to prove them wrong. I chose to say, "I'll show you!" And I did. I made something of myself before I ever knew God. I refused to let their words pigeonhole me into a life I didn't want—a life full of lack like they had, with small-minded ideas about me.

I played rock music. I made a lot of money. I did a lot of things and went a lot of places, and the lack of my childhood was long gone. So, yes, I made it financially—I had all I wanted—but was I happy? *No.* I can't tell you how much of a disappointment it was to realize that money alone didn't make me happy.

You see, "life and that more abundantly" isn't housed in financial success alone—it's housed in the whole package that God offers to us through applying His Word. You can rise to success by trying to "get back" at people who said this or that about you, but it will not bring you peace in the end, even if you prove them all wrong. Why? Because success can't give something spiritual to you.

You can't get peace from a "thing"—and yet God's Word says He will richly give you all "things" to enjoy (1 Timothy 6:17). So, God's not against you succeeding in any way and being the best at what He's called you to do in life. But your heart needs to know that your success shouldn't be tied to "getting back" at those who said negative things to you.

When you make "Just you wait and see!" the driver in your quest to succeed in life, what you are really doing is giving *your* energy to *their* negativity. In fact, you are being driven by something that at its very nature is untrue and dark. Do you think it will be so satisfying if what propelled you to success was trying to outrun a lie someone told you years ago? You can do it, but I promise, it'll leave you empty in the end. And if you cling to it even after you've succeeded, it'll leave you bitter. You'll be like a hamster on a wheel—continually trying to win a race that can never be won.

You win when you choose God's way. You win when you choose God's Spirit. You win when you see that your race is between you and God, and the goal is to fulfill the calling on your life. The aim should be to do the things God has put on your heart, to enjoy all the many good things in life that God blesses you with, and to become more Christlike as you live your everyday life.

Regardless of the challenges, you don't have to succumb to them. You can become stronger, overcome the obstacles, and keep moving forward in the good life God has for you.

Do You Have Generosity of Spirit?

Generosity of spirit is one of the marks of a believer. I've seen that being generous has the power to break the lack mentality and create breakthroughs in life. For many people, if they've been told the wrong things about how life works in the spirit realm, and if they've had to scrape for every bit of goodness in the natural realm, the natural human tendency for some is to get stingy with whatever they get—spiritually, physically, or financially. But as believers, God calls us to rise above stinginess and be generous in spirit, no matter what we have materially.

Being a generous person shows who you are inside—it shows that you are living out of an abundant heart that is *not* ruled by fear of lack. It's something you can feel and others can see. A person who has an abundant mindset has an easier time asking God for "whatsoever" they desire—they know that He is an abundant God who richly gives them all things to enjoy.

The abundant life is a spiritual concept they believe and accept, and so they get what they ask from God more easily because their faith isn't clogged up with a "never enough" lack mindset. Doubt doesn't rule their heart. Abundant thinking creates abundant talking, and their actions are done in faith, too—they know that what they do will be a success, that everything they touch will prosper, and that God will help them no matter what bumps in the road might come up. They freely give because they understand the reciprocal system God put into place—they sow, they reap, they sow again, and so on. They recognize when blessings come, even the littlest ones, and thank God, giving Him glory for it all. The cycle of blessing is something they see as an inevitable part of the believer's life.

The generous nature of a believer is something the devil hates. He's an enemy of the abundant life because it is what Jesus came to give mankind—and he fights it ferociously because he does not want God's best for mankind. He doesn't want God's best for you. He wants you fixated on "not enough" and what you don't have so that you'll keep talking about it and producing more fear of lack.

The devil is a taker, a user, and an abuser. He's manipulative. Those who follow him and this world's system end up doing what he does, even if they didn't start out intending to—because fear and lack are a cycle, too. The mindset is so strong that even wealthy people often end up acting stingy, hoarding, and refusing to help others very much because they still have an "I don't have enough" or "I'll run out" mindset. The fear of losing something, whether it's money, power, respect, or prestige, drives them to do all sorts of things.

Jails are also filled with people consumed by a lack mindset. Grave mistakes can happen when people *think* they don't have what it takes to get what they want or what they need the right way. Many do really desperate and horrible deeds. They consider it a shortcut to getting around lack. Those crimes start in the mind—the mind that thinks it's lacking in some area, whether it's power, or money, or whatever.

The abundant mind knows they can have what they need and want the right way—and so generosity of spirit comes more naturally. No matter their situation, generous people talk, live, and work in the world in a different way. It's a more joyful way. It's a way of seeing the world around them. They know they can help and change things, and so they do.

Day by day, those believers with an abundant mindset are generous with themselves, their time, their energy, and whatever financial blessings God has given them. Why? Because they have faith that God will always provide seed to the sower, and they are a sower! They have faith that God will always reward their generosity, and He does. They know that as they "cast their bread on the water," more and more will come back to them, and it does (Ecclesiastes 11:1). An abundant mindset produces a generous nature—and it's rooted in *no* fear of lack. Let me tell you something, that is not just a good way to be; it's a God way to be!

When you know that God is limitless and that abundance is what Jesus came to give, you can put your faith out there and ask for more from God—you can give more, receive more, ask for "whatsoever," and so on. Goal to goal, you can go in the direction of your heart's desires much easier with an abundant mindset and with a whole lot less stress. God takes pleasure in your prosperity—and when you have an abundant mindset, you take pleasure in it, too.

Why Sacrifice What God Never Asked For?

People are so fixated on life being hard that they'll even do things God never asked them to do in order to get Him to move. I find that the church world in general is really good at sacrificing—but they have a real problem with doing what God said to do. In other words, they'd rather suffer hardship and sacrifice than obey.

Look at this verse in 1 Samuel 15:22: "*But Samuel replied, 'What is more pleasing to the Lord: your burnt offerings and sacrifices or your obedience to His voice? Listen! Obedience is better than sacrifice, and submission is better than offering the fat of rams*'" (NLT).

I want you to notice that even before the Ultimate Sacrifice (Jesus Christ) gave His life for all, it was more pleasing to God that we just obey Him—way more pleasing than any hardship or sacrifice people put themselves through.

It blows my mind how some believers would rather do just about anything than simply obey God. They'll give up things He never asked them to give up. They'll do things He never asked them to do. It's like they think they can win God over by doing things He never asked them to do—and *then*, after they suffer enough, He'll give them the answer to their prayers. That's not how it works! God isn't moved by need or suffering. God is moved by faith. If God was moved by need, He'd never get out of India. He's not, and like it or not, that is what the scriptures tell us. Faith in the Word moves the hand of God because faith in the Word moves things in the spiritual realm first—and also because faith in the Word repels the devil.

So, regardless of how "good" your "sacrificing" is, if God didn't ask you to do it, what's the point? It's always better to obey God. I honestly believe that if God's children (past, present, and future) would simply obey His Word and His voice more, there would be a lot less sacrificing and suffering in life.

Read Psalm 35:27 again: "*Let them shout for joy, and be glad, that favour my righteous cause: yea, let them say continually, Let the Lord be magnified, which hath pleasure in the prosperity of His servant.*"

There is so much revelation to be had in this verse. When I was reading it, the Lord told me to focus on the word *pleasure*. When you give God pleasure by obeying John 14:13-14 and asking for "whatsoever" in Jesus' name, the Father is glorified and the name of Jesus is magnified when you receive it.

Your prosperity is *pleasurable* to God—it makes Him happy, it blesses Him, and brings Him glory. Really think about that for a moment and then ask yourself this question, "Why *not* give your Father in Heaven pleasure?" Realize that you aren't the only one who is going to shout and smile when you receive what you are praying for, aiming at, and moving toward in faith. *God* is going to be happy, too!

If you struggle with even thinking this way, you have to just repetitively retrain your mind to the truth by quoting this verse or creating an affirmation based on this verse that says, "My prosperity *is* pleasurable to God!" Go ahead and name what it is that you desire. If it's material blessings, train yourself to see them not as materialism but as manifestations of your faith that bring *God* pleasure. So, whether it's a new car, a new home, a better job, your dream business, more clients, more sales, or more money in the bank, you can create a confession or affirmation that says, "God gets pleasure every time I drive this new car!" or "This new home is making God and me happy!" or "God smiles when my bank account gets bigger! He's bringing more to me, and both of us are being more blessed every day!" Do you see what I'm saying here?

Notice that word *continually* in Psalm 35:27—*"let them say continually"* means non-stop! You might ask how you can do that all the time, and the answer is to become a well-disciplined thinker. You can't shout for joy or be glad with your mouth about your own prosperity if you don't *think* you should be prosperous. Again, if this keeps coming up, you're going to have to hammer away at confessing the Word over your life.

What you repetitively hear will build faith inside of you—so don't flinch when you make your list of confessions.

Can Others Hear What You Don't Say? Can They See What You Won't Show?

Every time a thought arises that doesn't match the Word, remind yourself that God gets *pleasure* in your prosperity. Don't let religious ideas, other people, or even the devil try to give you a mind of lack—don't allow the lies of the world to surpass the truth of the Word in your own mind. As you work on your thoughts, you'll feel freer to speak. Beware of the language of hesitation. Just notice if that old fear tries to rise up again after speaking the Word. If that happens, just conquer it. Realize that it is just an old habit trying to claw its lack-filled fingers back into your life.

Remind yourself again, "God gets glory when I'm blessed! God gets pleasure when I'm blessed! I believe that I have what I asked of God. I know it's coming, and I love who I'm becoming as I lean on Him and have faith in His wonderful Word! My heart, my mind, and my life are testimony to God's love, goodness, and faithfulness to His Word."

Others can't hear what you don't say. Others can't see what you won't show. Your testimony of God's goodness begins in your thoughts, but it must make its way out of your mouth and into your everyday life—and that's how you can continually "say" and "let the Lord be magnified" like Psalm 35:27 says. That's how you become a living testimony.

Your words acknowledging what God has done for you matter. Your authenticity in sharing about it matters. Your bravery to say how good God has been to you because you *"favor His righteous cause"* is a force for good that magnifies the goodness of the Lord. Prosperity *is* God's will for you, and it brings Him *pleasure.*

So, decide today to become a disciplined thinker who does not hesitate to speak and live by the Word. Change your thinking about prosperity with the Word if others have led you wrongly in the past. Have faith in God. Honor God with your words of praise. He is good and your prosperity blesses Him. Don't hide the news of His goodness. Don't shy away from shouting for joy and being glad about what God's done and is doing for you. Speak it out and live it out! Let others know just how good God is to those who have faith in His Word and favor His righteous cause.

What Does It Mean to Be Persecuted for the Word's Sake?

There are a lot of haters in the world. I've met quite a few! But I can honestly say that I've met way more good people who honestly love the Lord and want to follow Him in truth. It's amazing how you remember the haters though. The mind seems to want to cling to those words others say to hurt you— and it can be a challenge to not get offended when people persecute you for the Word's sake.

What does it mean to be persecuted for the Word's sake? In some places in the world today, that means being tortured or even killed for the cause of Christ—there are people who are blinded by hate and literally loathe the goodness of Christ and His followers. They persecute Christians for the Word that they believe.

So, when somebody asks me if my feelings are hurt by what the media may say about me negatively, or if they hear about somebody talking smack about me in church circles…well, it's hard not to shake my head and say, "Is that all they got?" Really, when there are people being beheaded on the other side of the world for being a Christian, I don't think my "persecution" on the news is such a big deal. Besides, even if they blasted my name and lied about me all day long because I believe in prosperity—or because I'm prosperous—that is just par for the course.

The Word says the hundredfold return comes "with persecution." It makes it very plain that if you prosper big, you'll get some flack. So what! Now, that persecution…well, I'll just say that I know from experience that "Percy" ain't "cute!" Is it tough? Yes, it's tough to be attacked by people who just don't grasp God in the way that I do. I wish they understood. I hope they one day do! But I can't give up what I believe just to fit in with others. I surely can't cave in and give up my beliefs when other Christians around the world aren't giving up theirs. Some are paying the price with their lives for that choice.

Let's imagine your life when you get exactly what you are asking God for. If you have a big dream, a big vision, and want a lot of the "things" God promises He will freely give to you if you follow after Him, let's imagine what you'll do when others *see* what God has done in your life financially. Because let's face it, nobody has a problem with your spiritual growth.

They don't have a problem if you get healed by God. But they *definitely* have a problem when God blesses you and makes you prosperous. What are you going to do when God prospers you big and the jaws around you start flapping with insults?

What Are You Going to Do When They Start Flapping Their Jaw?

When you achieve your dream, when you receive all the "things"…what are you going to do if they start persecuting you for the Word you chose to believe? What then?

Don't think it's all roses. There are thorns in the flesh out there that might as well be complete bushes! Prickly people who either because of jealousy, envy, or some misguided sense of power simply don't want you to prosper in any way—they resent it. Remind yourself that people attack what they don't understand—and people with a limited mindset will always resent those who don't play the "limited mindset" game. I'm not playing their game. I'm going with God's Word and what He put on my heart, and I suggest you do the same.

Just take it as a given that when God prospers you, you'll likely get some backlash of some kind—because an abundant mind that accepts prosperity as God's will for their life will always encounter some kind of denial, dismissal, and disapproval from those with a lack mentality.

You know that you've been blessed by God when the devil starts flapping his jaw! You know that you're getting elevated when they start trying to bring you down low. The haters are everywhere, but so what—it's not what they say that counts; it's what you and God say, right?

Those who are *not* living according to the Word don't want you living prosperously in *God's* system—they want you living like they do, according to the world's system. Don't let them change you. Stand your ground. It's not their life; it's yours. The dream God gave you is yours, not theirs. The understanding you have, well, they just don't yet have it—pray for them that they will!

Praying for those who despitefully use you and blessing those who curse you is *hard* in the flesh, but *easy* in the spirit. When you realize the power behind doing that, you will nearly run to do it. If the world's "killing them with kindness" idea comes to mind, you are on the wrong track. Praying for and blessing those who are trying to hurt you isn't a manipulative way to get back at them—it's not about that at all. This is a spiritual concept Jesus taught that *works* inside of you to break the pain and to help you forgive them, to help you release their words out of your heart so that you can get up, wipe the tears, and keep on running with your vision.

Verbal attacks and persecution for the Word's sake can derail your progress if you let it consume your mind. Praying for those fools and blessing them is your ticket out of misery over whatever they said or did—it is a spiritual concept, a force, that really can set *you* free, even if they are still wagging their tongues about you. Like the scripture says, you'll be able to shake the dust off your feet and keep on walking when they don't accept you. Don't dust those feet off and start walking until you've sincerely gotten with God about them—until you've prayed for them, blessed them, and broken their "hold" on your heart. That is one tip I can give you that I promise works!

It's hard to get offended by people if you pray for them. It's hard to hold on to the hurt and anger when you start blessing them. It totally disarms the devil! It breaks something in you. Is it hard at the beginning? Oh, yeah, in the natural you want to kill them, so it's tough to even think about blessing them or praying for them—but I promise, if you can get over that hurdle in the beginning, you are going to see that the verbal persecution that comes with prosperity is no sweat off your back.

Just get to the point in your mind, before you even receive, that you will *not* be shocked if you get some flak for being prosperous or telling the truth about God. Decide now that your life, your joy, your peace, and your calm assurance in the Word is just too important to relinquish to the doubters and haters of the world.

Don't hesitate to have faith when God tells you to believe Him for something. Don't hesitate to give Him praise when you get it—in fact, start praising Him every day *before* you get it, and you'll get it quicker. I don't care how much persecution comes; just be the kind of believer who'd rather obey God's Word than believe the world's word.

Everything anybody says against God and His Word will pass away—not one of their hate-filled words will matter in the end. God's Word will *never* pass away. So why get all flustered over the temporary words of men and women? Why worry about what "they" say—even if it's on the news, on a blog, or in a book?

There are people who literally make a name off of trying to smear other people! There are people who get prosperous off of writing books *against* prosperity. That's what you call hanging on to traditions of men—falling into the ditches, like the blind leading the blind. The truth is that the Word of God is going to remain *long* after their words are forgotten.

In fact, any words that somebody says against you for believing the Word are dying the moment they are spoken. Yes, their words may hurt you for a moment, but they are temporary and *not* God's Word or God's heart. Their mean-spirited words do not really matter because only God's words will matter in the end—He is the One with eternity on His side. If you speak His words, you have eternity on your side, too. You will live *forever* in the prosperity and generosity of God, no matter what they say. So, why not start living in prosperity and generosity here, too?

What Motivates Some People to Discourage Your Faith and Dismiss Your Dreams?

I have been attacked for my belief that God is a good God, that He loves us and wants to see us prosperous in every way. The media, some of my friends, pastors I've known, and even some of those who I thought were the closest to me have turned on me simply because I outwardly show what God has done in my life. Can you relate? Something odd happens when you *show* what God has done for you—because showing blessings exposes the deep-rooted lies of the devil and sometimes brings out the worst in people, even "good people."

I don't believe in hiding wealth, because I'm not ashamed of what God has done in my life. Do you know where I come from? I was born in poverty. I was told so many negative things, I couldn't write them all here if I tried—and I don't want to try! Why? Because they were never true. They were lies of the enemy. *All* of us have something God has sent us here to do—and *all* of us have a way out of whatever lies the enemy tried to get us to believe, even if those lies were repeated from our very birth.

Why do so many people attack our faith and our dreams… even when they claim to love us, want the best for us, and believe that God saved us for a purpose? I don't believe it's always motivated by straight-up hate, but I do believe that it's motivated by a deep-rooted lie of the enemy that says, "God is not interested in your well-being, and He couldn't care less if you have anything more than the basics of life." If God takes pleasure in your prosperity, like the Word says, then that is a bold-faced lie.

What makes that lie so tantalizing? The *fear* that is attached to it. Fear motivates people to do and say things they'd never do if they weren't scared of prosperity. So, think of it like this: Not everybody who attacks your faith or your dreams even realizes that fear is motivating them to do it. Many people simply do not understand your faith. Many don't believe God loves them enough to take pleasure in seeing them doing well—thinking well, talking well, dreaming well, and living well. They don't believe in your dreams, or the vision you have for your life, because it's not *their* dream or vision. They resent anybody asking for the desires of their heart because they don't have the understanding, wisdom, or guts to ask God for their own desires. Some people just hate to see success if God has anything to do with it!

A lot of people who don't understand that God gets pleasure from our prosperity get irritated by any teaching that turns the tables on the traditional view of God. For thousands of years, the world has pushed the bold-faced lie that God is either non-existent or not interested in humanity. The Church has pushed the idea that God is an angry, divine force that is always ready and willing to hit you with a lightning bolt if you step out of line—even now, after Jesus has come and paid the price for us, they still hang on to the idea that we can never really please God enough.

So, when some people attack your faith, just realize that they are motivated by *fear*. Why are some people hell-bent on maintaining the status quo? Why do they want to keep you in your "place" so much? It's because they have a limited view of God and His Son, and they fear change. Your changes make them think about their lives and about the state of things as they are now. Most people *don't* do what it takes to reach their goals, and they sure don't have the faith to ask God for their "whatsoever."

Most people fear stepping out of the boat of religion to walk on the water with Jesus. People like the boat. It's comfortable. But God requires us to get a little uncomfortable—faith isn't comfortable to the flesh. Still, that's what faith requires. We step onto the water to follow the Lord because that's where *He* is—and we want to go where He is! We don't serve a status quo God! All of Jesus' life and ministry broke the status quo. Don't you think you'll break it, too, if you follow after the dreams and goals He's put into your heart?

God didn't give other people your vision. He didn't plant your desires in their heart. They've got their own, and they are responsible for them. You are responsible for yours. Let their words go, like water off a duck's back. Be thankful if someone encourages you. Recognize those with faith around you, and tell them you appreciate them—let the words of the others go in one ear and out the other.

Will some scoff at your reasons for wanting better? Yes. Will they try and use humiliation to get you to keep up with the status quo? They may. Will they try to use natural thinking to uproot your faith in God's limitlessness? Oh, yeah, they will...but who cares? The doors God opens, no man can shut. The desires God places deep in your heart, no man can steal... unless you let them into your heart and unless you give up.

Don't let *their* fear get inside *your* heart. Don't let them suck away your good future. Don't give up. Once your eyes are open and you see that they are just motivated by fear, you can be as "wise as a serpent" and as "harmless as a dove" as you are interacting with them (Matthew 10:16). You don't have to let one scoffing, negative word burrow its way into your heart. You are meant to go in the direction God has for *you*—and that is *not* in the direction of fear.

Do You Know Who the Most Vicious Opponents of Your Prosperity Really Are?

Do you ever wonder why the devil hates the prosperity of believers? Do you ever wonder why people who claim to not even believe in God are so angry about the fact that you do? Do you ever wonder why some nearly break their teeth grinding them when they see a believer who loves God, promotes his faith, and is prosperous? The reason is simple: The devil, and all those who fell from Heaven with him, hates whatever brings God *pleasure*, and they hate whatever gives God's people *power* in the earth.

Beyond the average human fear of change, there is a spirit that motivates some people to *hate* Christians—and especially

> **The devil, and all those who fell from Heaven with him, hates whatever brings God pleasure, and they hate whatever gives God's people power in the earth.**

hate Christians who are succeeding financially. Why? Beyond misguided beliefs about what God wants for His children here on earth, I believe it's because money itself has become a strong form of power on this planet—and they don't want believers having power. If God gets pleasure in your prosperity, do you really think the devil wants you to be abundantly prosperous? Do you really think those who are deceived by him and live according to this world's system want believers to be prosperous? No. Think about it.

What do believers who follow after God do with their money when they are very prosperous? Are they greedy, do they hoard their finances, or enjoy seeing others live lowly while they enjoy abundance? Believers who prosper while putting God first in their lives are interested in a *lot* more than just accumulating stuff—instead, they want to see spiritual change in the world, and the rise of true good everywhere in the world.

Believers send the Gospel around the world. Those who prosper invest into the cause of Christ in a greater capacity. They have more to give, and so they do—and that affects the output of evangelism, which means more hear about the goodness of Christ and accept His love, His mercy, and His grace. Prosperous believers who put God first are a great support to the foundations, churches, and ministries that affect people all around the world for good. They are *big* planters of good things in this world, helping to establish things like hospitals and schools, and they often give a lot toward various missions. They often fund the education of many others, create safehouses for those in need, and fight against homelessness or helplessness around the world. Nearly all of the largest organizations helping others tangibly are Christian. A lot of good comes out of the heart of believers, and so the greater the prosperity of a believer, the more good around the world is funded. The heart of God is love.

I was always a generous man, but as God began to bless me more, I was excited to be able to bless others even more. Giving and receiving is just a part of my life, and I enjoy it! I like to say that I'm addicted to giving, and God supports my habit. Even when I didn't have much at all, and a "night out" meant going to McDonald's with my wife, Cathy, and our young daughter for a burger, we decided we wanted to be givers more than we wanted that night out.

Whatever need I saw that God put on my heart to do, I tried to meet that need—but there came a time, as God blessed me, that I thought, *God, I want to do more than just meet a need. I want to grant a wish.* In other words, I was growing. As I prospered, my heart extended to meeting the desires of others.

When you are a prosperous believer, you can do more than meet a need; you can grant a wish and fulfill a desire. You can blow someone away with generosity and give God the glory all the while. You see, helping someone with bus fare is meeting a need, and it's a wonderful thing to do—but being able to buy that same person a car is fulfilling a desire, and that's pretty good, too! Helping someone who is struggling to pay their house note is an absolutely wonderful thing to do—but being able to pay off that person's house so they never have to pay the note again, just because you want to be a blessing, well...that is even better! Trust me, I know, I've done all this many times. Why? Because that's what prosperous believers who follow God's voice do—they meet needs, they meet desires, and they inspire others to do the same. It's like a blessing cycle that can't be stopped. You'd be surprised how infectious giving is. When you do it to someone, they tend to do it to someone else. It's wonderful!

Who in their right mind would *hate* to see all that happening? You know who. The people who attack Christian prosperity the most viciously are motivated by a *lot* more than just a misunderstanding of prosperity—I believe they are motivated by the devil, and that's why they try to sabotage Christians who believe in prosperity. They don't want any joy, any peace, and any prosperity you might have coming to you. The scriptures tell us in Ephesians 6:12 that we don't fight with flesh and blood, but with the spirits that motivate flesh and blood—powers we can't see because they are invisible to natural eyes, but whose effects we *can* easily see.

Just look at the evil in the world today. This didn't happen by accident. Even human frailty and human nature can't take credit for this mess! One of the most effective tactics of the devil is making sure people think he's not real—but as believers, we know that the devil is not only the enemy of God, but he is also the enemy of God's people.

For we wrestle not against flesh and blood, but against principalities, against powers, against the rulers of the darkness of this world, against spiritual wickedness in high places. Wherefore take unto you the whole armour of God, that ye may be able to withstand in the evil day, and having done all, to stand. Stand therefore, having your loins girt about with truth, and having on the breastplate of righteousness; And your feet shod with the preparation of the Gospel of peace; Above all, taking the shield of faith, wherewith ye shall be able to quench all the fiery darts of the wicked. And take the helmet of salvation, and the sword of the Spirit, which is the Word of God.

Ephesians 6:12-17

Evil exists, but no matter what kind of "fiery darts" fly in your direction, it is your *faith* that will shield you from true harm. It's your faith that will keep you from being wounded by their lies and attacks on your desires, your goals, and your character. When you are under attack from the enemy, just don't forget that he is not a flesh and blood enemy—you aren't fighting people, but the spirit that is motivating them. I like to say that principalities work through personalities! The attack isn't aimed at *you* so much as it is aimed at God.

Just think about this verse again in relation to the attacks on prosperity that are so common nowadays: *"Let them shout for joy, and be glad, that favour my righteous cause: yea, let them say* *continually, Let the Lord be **magnified**, which hath **pleasure** in the **prosperity of His servant**"* (Psalm 35:27). Do you think dark spirits want you to have more money to further the "righteous cause" of God? Do you think they want you shouting for joy, being glad, and able to "say continually" that the *Lord* is the one magnified in your prosperity? Do you really think they want you having more money to promote God's "righteous cause"? Think about it.

The devil and the spirits who are with him don't want believers shouting for joy and magnifying God—they want us crying for help and running for cover! They don't care how long we stay at the altar, so long as we don't get up, go home, and actually start doing the work and will of the Lord on this earth. They don't want us magnifying God at all—not with our mouth and not with our money.

The devil hates God—and so the devil and all his fallen cohorts hate when you are prosperous. When you're blessed, you not only bring pleasure to God in Heaven, but you also bring *attention* to God's power right here on earth. Your joy brings attention. Your gladness, your support of the righteous cause, and your words that magnify the Lord—all of that garners attention! The devil likes a poor Church because he likes an ineffective Church.

So, if others go on the attack, just remember that you've already won because Jesus beat the devil when He went to the cross. Colossians 2:15 tells us that Jesus disarmed the spiritual rulers and authorities of this world and made a public spectacle of them when He triumphed on the cross. Even though Satan himself sometimes masquerades as an "angel of light," Jesus has already won and beaten him—so all his attacks will be futile in

YOUR **EVERYTHING** IS HIS **ANYTHING**

the end. Guess what? They can be futile in your life today, too, because *you* are part of the body of Christ and you have power over the devil and every single principality, power, might, and dominating spirit that motivates people to attack your faith. When Jesus beat the devil, He beat him royally—that idiot has no ranking that can even compare to Jesus Christ. Read this passage and realize that *you* stand with Christ.

> *That the God of our Lord Jesus Christ, the Father of glory, may give unto you **the spirit of wisdom and revelation** in the **knowledge of Him**: The eyes of your understanding being enlightened; that ye may know what is the **hope of His calling**, and what the **riches of the glory of His inheritance in the saints**, And what is the **exceeding greatness of His power to us-ward who believe, according to the working of His mighty power**, Which He wrought in Christ, when He raised Him from the dead, and set Him at His own right hand in the heavenly places, **Far above all principality, and power, and might, and dominion, and every name that is named, not only in this world, but also in that which is to come**: And hath put all things under His feet, and gave Him to be the head over all things to the church, Which is His body, the fulness of Him that filleth all in all.*
>
> Ephesians 1:17-23

So, the attacks aren't always "natural," but you've got Jesus with you, and now you don't have to be caught off guard by attacks from the enemy. Once you know that people who are most viciously opposed to your prosperity are that way *because* they are motivated by a spirit that doesn't want *God* to have pleasure, you won't be caught off guard by their attacks. You won't be surprised when they deny your right to be blessed, dismiss your faith as heresy, or vehemently disapprove of *your* prosperity. You won't even be upset with the person!

When you see that attack coming much too viciously, you'll know that the problem is spiritual. You know how to handle that! Pray. Use the Word. Speak the Word as if it is a sword, because it is! Let the Word coming out of your mouth do the work in the spiritual realm, and don't fight that person. Never forget that it is sad, but true, that some people are pawns in a game they don't even know they're playing! Pray for them, too, because they need it.

You are bringing God pleasure with your blessings—through your prosperity, you are magnifying God, glorifying God, and giving the devil fits, too. While the devil doesn't really care about your stuff so much, he sure does care about your testimony. He sure cares about your influence. He might get all riled up when you bring attention to God, but do it anyway. Share God's goodness and generosity anyway. Be joyful. Open your mouth and be glad knowing that God has amazing things in store for you, and the devil only fights what he fears.

Did You Know That Desires of the Heart Follow Joy in the Lord?

Joy is a powerful way to crush negativity—and that's why you do all you can to not let what the devil or anybody else says get in your heart and ruin things. Breakthroughs can happen just by choosing joy—because the Bible tells us that desires of the heart follow delighting in the Lord.

"**Delight** *thyself also in the Lord; and He shall give thee the* **desires** *of thine heart*" (Psalm 37:4). This shows that you can bless the Lord so much that He'll just give you what you want— He'll just drop desires right on you as you're going along your way in life. He won't be able to help Himself because He will be so blessed by the way you delight yourself in Him. God does this to me all the time. This isn't just about putting Him first in life. It's about doing it with *joy* that comes from the heart. They didn't use that word *delight* for nothing!

When you delight yourself in the Lord and His way of doing things, it blesses Him so much that He just *gives*. Notice that He doesn't give you challenges in return for delighting yourself in Him. He doesn't give you misery. The Lord gives one thing according Psalm 37:4, and that's *desires* of the heart. Think about that!

So, while you delight yourself in the Lord, it causes Him to give you the desires of your heart, which makes you prosperous in some way, which brings Him pleasure…and you return the favor by, again, delighting yourself in Him…which causes Him to give to you again and again. I know that's a long sentence, but do you see the cycle? Do you get how *good* God is?

This is a *relationship* we have with the Lord! It's a joyful relationship, a good relationship, a solid and delightful relationship. Out of that delight comes a cycle of giving and receiving—from God's heart to yours, from the spirit realm to the natural realm. It's a cycle of goodness, joy, and blessing! Love *gives*. Love takes delight in *receiving*. God *is* Love. When you delight in Him, you become more like Him—you can't help but give, you can't help but delight when He gives back to you. When you start to see that your own heart desires are connected to the delight you have just by being with Him and by following His goodness, you'll see how important it is to let go of those distractions of life that aren't taking you anywhere that matters very much.

Where do you want to go in life? What do you want to do? What blessings do you want to enjoy? What breakthroughs do you desire to have? Focus on *joy*—on delighting yourself in the Lord. You'll see that as you do, *all* those desires will come to pass and you'll enjoy yourself a whole lot in the process, too!

CHAPTER NINE

Why Would Anyone Deliberately Limit God?

Have you ever asked yourself why anybody in their right mind would deliberately put limitations on God? I mean, what pleasure do people get in limiting God or trying to limit others? And yet people did it in the Old Testament and the New Testament. Even today, people seem to constantly want to put limits on God, others, and even themselves! It's sad but true.

Let's look at one example found in Psalm 78:41: *"Yea, they turned back and tempted God, and limited the Holy One of Israel."* With all the miracles the children of Israel saw, including all their enemies destroyed, they still limited God. The church world does that even to this day. Again, it's sad but true. People will say things like, "That can't be true" when you believe what the Bible says in John 14:13-14: *"And **whatsoever** ye shall **ask** in My name, that will I do, that the Father may be **glorified** in the Son. If ye shall ask **any thing** in **My name**, I will do it."* What are these people doing? They're calling Jesus a liar—and like Psalm 78:41, they are *turning back* from belief in the words of Christ and with their very own mouth, they are *limiting the Holy One of Israel.* Whoa! I know that's strong, but it's true.

Who are we to dismiss the words of Christ, no matter how unbelievable to the natural mind some of His words may be? Who are we to put limits on the Holy One of Israel by doubting and dismissing His will and/or ability?! While most believers aren't comfortable calling Jesus a liar, many do just that with their hearts when they dismiss Jesus' teachings and deny God's ability.

Just as sure as the serpent in the Garden deceived Adam and Eve into thinking that God's word to them wasn't true, the devil will try to deceive *you* into thinking Jesus' words aren't true either. Refuse to be like those who *"turned back and tempted God, and limited the Holy One of Israel."*

Are You Willing to Emancipate Yourself from Limited Thinking About God?

Israel never experienced God's best and never even got to see how far God could take them because they had narrow thoughts about God. They limited God in many ways, but they all stemmed from dismissing or denying something God said. Again, same old devil, same old schemes! If he can get you to dismiss or deny the truth, he'll keep you living lowly—spiritually, physically, financially, or in all three areas together!

We should never allow petty and inadequate ideas about God to remain in our mind. That's why I'm always saying, "Believe the unbelievable and receive the impossible because it's doable." You see, I've decided *not* to dismiss or deny God's Word. I refuse to have small ideas about God! Why? Because I don't want a small life!

Abundance is personal, and we all have a different idea of what prosperity or a successful life looks like. Success means different things for everyone—but each of us was created to do something here on earth that matters. With God, no matter what your goal, your dream, or the vision you have for your life, it's doable—and it's *big* in His eyes. Don't have a narrow view of success! A woman who owns a company that sells millions of products isn't any more "successful" than a woman who stays home and raises her children wonderfully—if each fulfilled the desire God put in their heart, then each one is doing well and thinking *big!*

Success is doing what God called *you* to do. Success is living *His* way as you go, with faith in Him and yourself—and without accepting the limits of fear and doubt. You will never have a big life with a small idea of God. Have faith in God's limitless ability to help you fulfill your dreams, goals, and desires. Doubt arises when you feel unsure, but don't allow it to remain. Let it go and choose faith. Don't be narrow-minded about what God can and can't do—He can do anything, including "whatsoever" we ask in His Son's name. There is no reason for us to limit God with doubt in His Son's teachings. Again, why on earth would we want to do that?

We have to train our minds not to doubt. We have to see it as just a "natural" way of thinking that won't get us where we need to go. Have you ever been driving somewhere that you've never been? You feel kind of apprehensive as you go along, don't you? You hope you're going the right direction. Faith trusts the Holy Spirit within. Faith says, "Even though I'm doing something new, something I've never done, I know that You put it in my heart, God. I am speaking Your Word, and I know that You are with me every single step of the way. You are my guide! You are my Lord! I'm on an adventure in faith, and I let go of all doubt in You."

Faith is what being a believer is all about. It's what being a disciple of Christ is all about. We can't entertain lies and expect to walk in truth. Remember, that's why a disciplined thought-life is what the Word so often encourages us to develop. It's up to you to choose God's timeless truth over our temporary thoughts. The more you do it, the more you are bending your will to God's will and conditioning your natural mind to reverence God for who He is—*limitless* in every way.

When you limit God and think small, you will end up with littleness of life, narrowness of outlook, and meagerness of power—it's a poverty mindset that infects all areas of your life because limited thinking is always focused on lack of some kind or another. Instead of looking at God's promise, the impoverished mind thinks about the problem so much that it overwhelms their faith. Impoverished thinking will steal your faith, destroy your vision, and rob you of the future God wants for you—why would you want to railroad your own future by limiting God in your own mind? You must emancipate yourself from all limited thinking when it comes to what God wants to do for you.

Do You Put Limits on God's Love?

Never, and I mean never, put limits on His love! Most people don't have faith in God because they have put limits on His love—and out of that limited thinking, they cannot move into believing God for health, prosperity, or anything they really desire because, in their heart, they do not believe God really loves them. They do not believe they are enough. Oh, they know Jesus died for their sins, but they still walk around as if every sin they've ever committed is being held over their head by God. *No!* This is guilt and shame clinging to a believer who is supposed to be free, but its root is in the belief that God's love has limits.

The love of God is limitless. If you struggle with this, you need to build your faith in the truth that God *is* love—He is good, He sent His Son out of love for *you*, and His Son washed your sin away. *Wash!* That means you are clean. *Away!* That means whatever "it" is, it's no longer attached to you in any way, any shape, or any form anymore. You are *clean* before God—and you didn't earn more of His love by getting washed in the blood. You were loved even when you were thinking and living in opposition to God. He loved you when you were yet a sinner.

The cross brought you back to God—not the other way around. Remember that in the beginning, God didn't choose to leave man; man made a freewill choice to leave God. That was a denial of God's love playing itself out. What did God do? He still loved. He loved the world so much that He gave His only begotten Son.

The blood of Jesus was shed as an act of love. Now, all of us can look at the cross and see just how far God went to prove His love to us. What did He want back? The same thing He wants now. God wants to welcome His children back home so that they can receive His love, know His mercy and grace, and walk in the abundant blessings of knowing Him.

> Expect **that whatsoever you ask in His name will come, and that it will bring glory to God. Never put limits on His love, His claims, His purposes, and His power!**

The love of God pulses in His Word. It flows through His Holy Spirit. It was made manifest in Jesus Christ. God's love is not only for salvation though—it's for *all* areas that are available to us as believers. God sent His Son not only to die for us, but to teach us what to do when we have desires in our life. We must obey Him and *ask*—not in doubt, but in faith that He will do it. "Whatsoever" in John 14:13 covers everything, whether it's spiritual, physical, or financial, etc. Our *everything* is His *anything!*

Is Somebody Lying?

Expect that God's Word is so good that it will always work on your behalf. *Expect* that the desires of your heart will come to pass. *Expect* that whatsoever you ask in His name will come, and that it will bring glory to God. Never put limits on His love, His claims, His purposes, and His power!

Think about what Israel did. God brought them out of bondage, He divided the Red Sea for them, and He guided them by a cloud and by fire—He even caused rocks to give them water! And yet they sinned against Him and limited Him. Now, how dumb is that? Jesus gave us the power of attorney to use His name, and yet most of the Church world won't do it.

Many don't believe that healing is for today, and yet Jesus was a healer in His earthly ministry and the Word tells us that stripes were laid on His back for our healing—which means healing is God's will. Many also think poverty is good and prosperity is bad, and yet the Bible is filled with stories of overflow miracles, abundant blessings, and the favor of God on His people—which means God has no problem with us being blessed. In fact, Psalm 35:27 expressly tells us that God takes *pleasure* in our prosperity.

Jesus is the same yesterday, today, and forever, partner. We can be blessed in the city, blessed in the field, blessed coming in, and blessed going out. And if somebody says we can't, well... *somebody* is lying and it isn't Jesus! It's just somebody with a limited view of God who doesn't realize the truth yet. Don't adopt their limited thinking.

Do You Limit God to Only One Day a Week?

Never limit God to just Sunday, and never forget that your home is His house, your office is His house, even the playground is His house—because He is everywhere, and He's in you! Every day is His day. He is the Lord of our whole life, so don't relegate Him in your mind to just one place or one measly day.

I don't just think about God on Sunday because it's the typical church day. I know you don't either. As believers who love Him and want the best life He has for us, we are committed to acknowledging Him, serving Him, and spreading His goodness 24/7. Our salvation is not a bunch of starts and stops or fits! Our salvation is strong and steady, and so we can *live* strong and steady, too. We can take *every* day as an opportunity to establish His kingdom right here on earth.

Inside my heart, this message of "Your Everything Is His Anything" is just getting bigger and bigger…I want to shout so loud right now, "DON'T LIMIT GOD!" You see, your life can't be God's best (it can't be "big" in the areas you desire) if you limit Him to one section of your heart, your mind, or your life. For me, it's all or nothing with the Lord—and I choose *all*. He is my "all in all" and there is nothing gray about it. I encourage you to live the same way, because it's a better way—His way, all the way, and every day!

Don't let the Church or anybody else trick you into treating His timeless truth as if it's over and finished—no! God's Word is a living, growing, and ever-expanding truth. It's not only what guides us as believers, but it's what breaks the yoke, lifts us up, and sets us free—spiritually, physically, financially, and in just every single way that we allow it to rule and reign in our lives. Everything we need or desire, or could ever desire, will come as we faithfully put His truth first, follow it, and "ask anything" in His name! Our "everything" really is His "anything"—let's put our faith forward and be brave enough to ask.

CHAPTER TEN

Will You Give God Honor?

"...for them that honour Me I will honour...."
1 Samuel 2:30

People seem to always ask me things like, "Brother Jesse, how do you know what to do with the ministry God's given you? How do you know what is the right direction for both the ministry and your own life?" I tell them the truth. It's not that hard and, really, it's pretty simple. I honor God first. I listen to His voice. I value His Word above everything else.

You see, I know that His Word is the last word; it's a light and a lamp unto my path. There is nowhere I can go that God doesn't go with me, of course—but I'm not interested in doing things my own way and looking for God's stamp of approval. I'm interested in doing things His way and gaining His divine honor! When God honors you, it's a form of divine favor. I need that to fulfill my destiny and reach my destination, and you do, too.

Some people don't consult with God on the little things. They don't acknowledge the presence of the Holy Spirit, who is with them 24/7. But I promise that if you are faithful in honoring God by listening to His still, small voice and putting

His Word above your own, He will make you ruler over more than just little things—He will bring you to a place of *much*.

Blessing follows those who honor God. Favor follows those who honor God. Don't get into the habit of just running to Him when you need answers for the big things. Make sure you honor Him in the little things—and that starts with just your morning routine, your habit of praying within yourself during the day, and as situations come your way. Acknowledging His powerful and all-knowing presence is step one!

Are You Honoring God?

You are capable of receiving everything you need and desire from God—because you are a person of faith and you serve a generous God. The generosity of God is demonstrated in the lives of people throughout the Word who honored God—their stories are inspirational and show us that when God said, *"for them that honour Me I will honour,"* He meant it. It's a promise. When you honor God, He pays you back in honor. He sees when you live with integrity. He sees your heart, your intentions, and your efforts to honor Him in your daily life.

There is a generation that is coming up after us—and we lay the foundation for them when we honor God outwardly as we live our lives, and not just when we are alone and talking to Him in private in prayer. I believe that what we've been given must not only work for us, but must also be passed on to the next generation. And why is that? Because we are trustees of this faith in His name—and we must know and pass on the fact that *everything* we ask in His name is only possible because we are carriers of His name. The anointing rests on Jesus, and when we are united with Him the anointing rests on us, too. We must use His name with purity and faith and never make an excuse for it.

As I've said, I will never make an excuse for the blessings of God in my life. You see, I don't care what the world likes or doesn't like about God's spiritual, physical, or financial blessings in my life. Pleasing people isn't my goal. I couldn't do it if I tried! But bringing glory to God and honoring God, well, that is easy—that I can do! It's something you can do, too.

Ask yourself, do others see you honoring God in public? Do they hear you saying good things about God? Do they see you believing the best, aiming for the best, and honoring both God and other people as you go about your day? If you have children, do you tell them about the goodness of God— or do they hear more complaining about life's injustices, inconveniences, and problems?

I believe our children can't just hear about the Gospel, but they must see its effects on our life. They can't just hear that they can have a good life, but they need to see us modeling a good life, too. We are all connected and we learn from each other—I believe that it's our job to lift one another up instead of tearing each other down. It's our job to honor the God who loves us, and do it both in our house and in public...not just at church.

Are You a Blessing in a World of Takers?

You stand out like a light in a dark world—somebody who believes in blessing others and receiving from others. Like breathing in and out, we sow and we reap, and we do it again and again in all sorts of ways. To be a blessing in a world of takers is what we, as believers, are meant to do.

I've said it many times, "The only Jesus some people may ever see is the Jesus in you or the Jesus in me." Every time we show the love of Christ, we are honoring God's love. Every time we see someone hurting and help, we are honoring the mercy and care of God.

Every time we honor the dream of our own heart and run with the vision God has given us—and we talk about it, show what's happening, and share our story—we are honoring the God who gave us those dreams. We are also inspiring others to go for their own dreams and desires, too. Being a light in the world is a good thing!

A lot of people "play fast" in this world—in other words, they don't do things right and instead live as takers without any care for God or other people. The world is full of takers who don't honor themselves, much less God. In the end, they cheat themselves out of a good life by not being honorable—because what a man sows, that shall he also reap (Galatians 6:7). It works both in the direction of good and in the direction of evil.

Show others what it means to be a blessing, a giver, and a receiver—show them what it means to be a blessing in a world of takers. Your life will stand out by contrast, God will get the glory, and you will receive honor for being honorable.

Have You Noticed Those Who "Play Fast" with God's Principles?

How would you like it if every time someone came around, they only came for what you could give them? What if they only talked to you when they wanted something? What if they never considered you, looked at you, or spoke to you…even when you were right there in the same room? Yet many people who say they love God do just this thing—they "play fast" with the principles of the Word. They don't really care about honoring God, they are only in it for what they can get. That's just a Christian version of a taker, and it's no good.

People can also play fast with the principles of God by living in a constant state of wavering in doubt. Everyone has doubts that come up. That's the normal human mind trying to wrap itself around something it's either never thought about or experienced before—that's just natural thinking. We all have doubts that temporarily arise, but a believer's life is marked by a choice to believe God's Word.

Experiences in life may give you one thought process, but it's the Word that gives you the truth. So, if you are a believer and choose to constantly doubt God and play devil's advocate all the time, you are just playing games with the truth you claim to believe. Playing games with God doesn't get you anywhere. Nothing He says works if you don't believe or apply it. The

believer's life is faith mixed with patience and perseverance—
and the goal is to become more like Christ.

Indifference or disregarding the truth that you know is
also playing fast with the principles of God. So, if a person
says they believe but doesn't even bother having faith in God,
he can't expect results—because you can't play fast with God's
principles and get results.

It's dishonorable to God to ignore Him or disregard the
truth you know, and it's also dishonorable to never talk about
what He's done for you. Doing these kinds of things not only
affects you and your future but also affects countless others
who are watching, listening, and could be inspired by you.

If you find that you lose faith often, guess what? So does
everyone else! Faith doesn't "stack up." Faith comes by *"hearing,
and hearing by the word of God"* (Romans 10:17)—it doesn't
come by "heard." What you heard last week, last year, or for
the past 50 years won't give you all the faith you need. You
can't hear inconsistently and expect to have enough faith for
whatever comes up in your life. You must replenish what you
use—that's why the Bible tells us faith comes in a present tense
way, which means it doesn't store up or stack up in your mind.
Faith is in constant flux. The more you use it, the more you
need to replenish your own faith by *"hearing, and hearing by the
word of God"* again.

Do You Honor God Out of Love or Fear?

While some people don't follow God and live a taker's life,
others follow God's statutes intently—but only out of fear.

Would you be pleased if your children flinched at your voice every time they came to see you? Would it make you feel good to see them cower in your presence, as if you were an abusive parent?

There is a big difference between reverencing God for who He is (and praising Him for it) and shrinking in His presence because you think He is going to harm you. God loves you! He is a good Father! Yes, there is a judgement side to God, but if you obey Him you'll never see it—and besides that, once you receive Christ, your sins are washed away and never to be remembered against you anymore. You are justified in Christ. You're not appointed to His wrath but to His grace.

If you struggle with this, focus on relaxing in your position in Christ. Relax in the truth that you have power and you have authority—and God loves you with His whole heart. He's not looking to take something from you, but give something to you.

Claim your rightful place as His loved child. Get comfortable in God's love for you so that you can obey His Word with an open heart that has no fear of God's intentions toward you—and His intentions are good! Your focus needs to be on what's good, and it's hard to do that if you are constantly worried about displeasing God. Your faith in God is what pleases God. He will help you live right, of course, but it's His will that you enjoy your life with Him—not fear for your life with Him. You are loved without limits!

That's why Jesus wasn't afraid to tell you to ask *anything* in His name in John 14:13-14—He wasn't telling you to approach the Father with foreboding…He was telling you to

YOUR EVERYTHING IS HIS ANYTHING

go where there are no *limits. "And whatsoever ye shall ask in My name, that will I do, that the Father may be glorified in the Son. If ye shall ask any thing in My name, I will do it."* The principle is that you can "ask anything" because you serve Someone who can do it and will do it!

You shouldn't shrink back in fear and think that's honoring God—because honoring God is about obeying His Word and heeding the Holy Spirit within you (both of those are only for your own good). God gets the pleasure of seeing you prosper as a result. Like a good Father, He gets to enjoy seeing His children living their dreams, conquering their challenges, and spreading love and joy with others.

We please God when we listen to His wisdom. Of course, He will help us climb out of the ditches of life if we fall into them, but I believe He would prefer it if we just listen to Him and obey the wisdom of His Word. We honor Him as our Father when we do. Our obedience displays that we *know* He knows what He's talking about!

Are You a Grateful Believer?

Have you ever held a door open for someone who didn't say thanks? Have you ever helped someone who later never acknowledged your help? Just like it's honorable to acknowledge what others do for you, it's honorable to acknowledge what God has done for you, and not just privately, but publicly. Your words bring Him glory and honor, and your praise is important not only for His ears, but for all who hear you.

Honoring God shows character, and the more you do it the more grateful you become—which induces joy for everyday living. It's hard to stay in the dumps when you are grateful. It has an opening effect to the heart, relaxing the mind and giving you a greater ability to see more of the good things that are already in your life. Gratitude moves the hand of God.

Do you remember the biblical story about the lepers who were healed by Christ? Do you remember that only one went back to say thank you, and that one was the only one who was made completely whole? The rest were healed, but the one who honored Christ with gratitude was made whole—in other words, his body wasn't just cleansed of the disease but the effects of having it were cleared away, too. That detail about thankfulness wouldn't be in the Word if it didn't matter!

Honor and gratitude are linked, and they matter. It shows character to stop, be grateful, and give honor where it's due, and God notices it. Not enough people do it, and many dismiss God's best because of that. When you wake up, wake up grateful. Be vocal about it. See where you are, even the nature that is around you—and acknowledge God with gratitude for what He has created. You will always enjoy life more when you appreciate what's around you. The people He has put into your life are worth being grateful for. The things you have that make your daily life better are worth being grateful for. Even the grass on the ground, the birds in the air, the waves on the sea, and the amazing things that we often see every day and take for granted are worthy of appreciation.

Gratitude also affects your ability to follow God's statutes. I believe that the person who cleaves to God will always honor God in their daily conduct—because there is something about gratitude that keeps you in check. It's not hard to live the saved life. You should start to see gratitude as a helper for your mind—it'll help keep you in check because it's hard to go against the goodness of God when you are grateful for what He's done.

You may have heard me say it before, but I decided a long time ago that I would create my world and live in it—and part of "creating my world" is staying grateful. I consider it a form of honor to say thank you to God and to people for whatever they have done for me.

Gratitude is something all people appreciate. There is just something inside of us that feels good when we are appreciated—when what we've done is acknowledged as good. I believe that even God appreciates hearing "thank you!" So, thank Him for His Word. Be generous with your words. I firmly believe that God will not hold back in giving generously to you if *you* don't hold back in generously honoring Him—and gratitude is a wonderful way to honor His goodness in your life.

Thank God in private for what He's done, but I encourage you to also go out into the world and brag on Him in public, too. God enjoys it and people *need* to hear the good things He's done. It inspires them to look around and be grateful, too.

Do You Realize Your Story Is Important?

Tell your story. Any area that God has touched your life, helped you, or shown you a better way to think or live—that is part of your life story. When you share where you've come from and where God has taken you, you are shining a light in a dark world. You honor God when you refuse to hide your light. You honor Him when you tell your story.

When will you give God honor in this way? Why not today? It's not hard. If you've heard me preach, you probably already know that I believe it's great to brag on God—I mean, why not? He brags on us believers in the Word all the time. He's always saying how wonderful we are in one way or another. He lavishes good words on us. We should lavish good words on Him. God is serious about honor. You should be, too.

In fact, take His good words about you as a tip for how to handle your relationships. Words matter. Not everybody cares about words as much as some do, but everybody needs to be acknowledged with gratitude now and again—everybody. Some need your words more than others. When you see that, give people the gratitude they need. You'd be surprised how little gratitude they may have experienced in their life. God sees this.

We say good things to children all the time and have no problems with it. We see them light up. Just because somebody is grown, hard as nails, or super-competent, don't think that they don't need to hear something good—in fact, they may need it more than anybody! Kindness solves a lot. Every kind or encouraging word you say matters. Realize that you honor God when you honor others. Do this as unto the Lord and just see how it affects not only the moods of others, but your own mood as well.

What you say is revealing something about you—so what are you saying? Some people say, "But I don't have a story, Brother Jesse." Yes, you do. We all do. Every day we are creating our lives by our choices and our words. We are living in our own story, why not live on purpose? What we say about ourselves, our lives, and God has an effect on our day, and it has an effect on others, too. What are they hearing when they hear from you?

What's the Focus of Your Story?

When I was growing up, I went to churches whose focus was on the problem. They'd ask people to stand up and "testify for the Lord," and they'd spend ten minutes talking about every single thing that went wrong, and two seconds saying, "But, praise God, He brought me through!" I'd always leave those services feeling worse than when I got there!

The details of your story matter—and they tell a lot about whether you honor God or you honor problems. Yes, you can tell the good, the bad, and the ugly parts of your story, but don't forget to tell the *best* part—the God parts! Where is "Jesus" in your story when you are talking to others about your life? When you are sharing your testimony, do you talk about what turned it around for you? Where you turned to God, where you obeyed, and where you had more faith in what He could do than what you could do on your own—those are key elements in a testimony, and people need to hear that!

Anybody can complain about a problem, but if God has seen you through it, why not give God the glory and honor that He deserves by shifting your focus to His power in your life? Listen to how you talk—notice where you "land" the most and where you want to "camp out" in your story. That's a good indicator of what you need to bring to the Lord and where your mind tends to go on its own, but that is not always the best place for your mind to be. Make it a point to start re-looking at your story and really honing in on Jesus and the good that came out of it all. That's the best part of any story!

Maybe you went through a bad sickness or disease, but are you still here? Ha! Have you stopped breathing? No. Maybe you were in dire straits, but have you come out of it? Maybe you were in an abusive relationship but God was with you and gave you the strength and courage to see yourself for who you really are, and you made it out—glory! God is our deliverer, our healer, and the rescuer of so many. So when you think of your story, which is more weighty in your mind—the challenge or the victory?

If you are still here on the planet, that means it was not your time to go, and you have more to do and more to tell—that means you have options! Options and opportunities are ahead of you, not behind you. Your story is continuing, and you are getting better and better. You're getting better at thinking well of yourself, believing God's best, having faith in God's Word, and living your life well. Every challenge that didn't take your life is a challenge you beat—and if you turned to God, you didn't beat it on your own. Acknowledge God's part in rescuing, saving, and guiding you. Honor Him for who He is, and look ahead with faith that wherever you are going is better than where you came from—even if you are on top now, you are destined to ascend even further!

Are You Looking Ahead or Back?

I'm in my "winter years" as you may have heard me say, but I'm doing more now than when I was young. I'm being more effective in my calling, and I'm having a better time at it than I ever have. I'm a man of vision. While most of the people I started out preaching with are retired, I'm still going strong—and I seem to be going faster even. I'm not content to go and lay on a beach somewhere. It's not in my nature. God has given me a purpose and a calling that energizes me. I'm looking ahead, not back. Like Paul, I'm forgetting those things which are behind and looking forward to those things that lie ahead. I'm pressing toward the mark of the high calling of God in Christ Jesus (Philippians 3:13-14).

So, if I think about my past, I don't look back with regret. My focus isn't on any of the mistakes or troubles that have been thrown in my path over the course of my life thus far. I can remember them. I may recount them as part of my story. Nobody's life is a perfectly straight road, and life throws curve balls. But my focus isn't on the past—it's on where I'm going next. If I look back, I look back only in order to honor God for where He's brought me from. My default mentality is that I'm looking forward to where I'm going next! I'm enjoying today. I'm creating my tomorrows today with the faith I have in God's Word. That's a blessed life!

How do you want to live? How much joy or peace do you want? It's connected to how much of the Word you want to believe and live—like me, you are creating your future today. So, decide how you want today to be. Look at where you're going, in your mind as much as in your life. I always say that if your memories are bigger than your dreams, you've got a problem—but it's one you can fix today. Look *up* first; God is with you. Look ahead; there's more for you to do. Realize that the Holy Spirit is in you to not only help you achieve the long-range goal but the short-range joy!

The Holy Spirit can help you have the bravery to ask God for what you need while you have the faith to receive it. You can make this day a good day, if that is what you really want. The Holy Spirit is *in* you and can help you put your eyes where they need to be—ahead! And when you do look at your past, the Holy Spirit within you can help you to see it all in a brand-new light—one that brings you greater perspective and more joy and brings greater honor to God and His power in your life.

Are You Tapping into the Boldness Available to You?

My wife was so quiet and shy when we met. Later, after we married, she was quiet and shy everywhere but in the house! She was saved before me, went to church all the time, and was always crying at "testimony time." After I got saved, I'd go with her and watch her raise her hand to testify at church, and then get up and just start bawling and squalling. She couldn't get a word out. It would touch her heart to retell what God had done for her, and she'd cry—but I don't really know if she could've gotten a sentence out even if she wasn't crying! Why? She just was plain shy.

But guess what? Today my wife, Cathy, is a pastor! She speaks with boldness and authority, and even if you tried, you couldn't keep her quiet about the things of God. I've seen firsthand how boldness can come upon even the shyest of people when they step into their rightful position. Cathy calls it "stepping into your yes"—which means stepping into the place of obedience to what God has put on your heart to do. It often requires you to be more than you thought you naturally were capable of being. That's good! That's growth! Out of obedience, courage comes to help you do what you must do.

Boldness is something that comes on us by way of the Holy Spirit—they don't call it the fire for nothing! Read the story about the Upper Room and see what happened when the Holy Spirit fell on the people. Languages changed. People were able to share the story of Jesus Christ with others who didn't even speak their language—the Holy Spirit is powerful and mysterious! This unusual and sovereign phenomenon changed the world as we know it because this was the beginning of mass evangelism after Jesus' death on the cross and resurrection. Suddenly, people who were meek and fearful became bold and outspoken about Christ. These were not angels; they were people like you and me.

Boldness came upon those in the Upper Room, and they were compelled to go out of that room and start talking about what Jesus had done. Are you bold enough to say what Jesus has done? The Holy Spirit can help you to grow in this area. He has not stopped giving people what they need in order to do what they've been called to do—and we've all been called to *do the work of an evangelist,* which means we've all been called to talk about Jesus Christ and Him crucified (2 Timothy 4:5). It takes courage to be outspoken, but this world needs people who are brave and courageous enough to publicly talk about Christ.

When you honor God in this way, you do so to your own salvation—as in, it saves you from a lot of trouble in life! How? Honoring God sets up the divine system of Him honoring you.

Honoring God is a gift that we give ourselves—because honoring God not only sets our mind in the right place but activates God's divine promise to honor us in return. Can you think of a better gift you could give yourself? Every time you sow honor, you can look forward to being honored. God is wonderful!

When you talk about God without shame, it encourages others who love God to put aside their shyness about His power in their lives. When you believe God for something and you get it, say that, too. I don't care if it's spiritual, physical, or financial—speak up. I know that you don't want to come across as a braggart—but if you have ever heard me speak, I know you know that I *believe* in bragging on *God!*

Remember that your salvation, healing, deliverance, blessings, relationships, whatever...none of that is about *you* and what you've done as much as it is about what Christ has done. It's His blood, His stripes on His back, His

> **Honoring God is a gift that we give ourselves—because honoring God not only sets our mind in the right place but activates God's divine promise to honor us in return.**

teachings, and His power! You just apply the Word and get what He has done—you apply the principles and receive the results of your faith in them. Once you get that deep inside, you won't have much trouble at all saying what He's done; it won't feel like bragging to you at all.

When you see that it is Jesus—what He's done and what He's said—and that it's only your faith in what He's done and said that is giving you the results, you will have a hard time *not* saying something about your blessings! Whether they are spiritual, physical, financial, or otherwise, the blessing of God's touch on your life will be burning in your heart and on your tongue. Out of the abundance of your heart, your mouth *will* speak.

Why Not Get into the Blessing Cycle?

You know, honoring God really does create a cycle of blessing. I love it when my daughter and granddaughter tell people what I do for them; it honors me as a father. I begin to honor them more; I can't help myself. It's like what God does when He said if you honor Him, He'll honor you—it's an honor and blessing cycle.

I believe that you are moving forward in your faith, and your desires are going to be met in Jesus' holy name. I believe that if you are committed to ask "whatsoever" and believe anything, like John 14:13-14 says, your Christianity will become a transmittable instinct. You will begin to affect so many more than you can imagine, just by living your life of faith and honoring God as you go.

When you commit to having childlike faith in Jesus' teachings—when you start asking for whatsoever you desire and living your best life, your faith becomes an "instinct" that rises up easily. Why? Because the Holy Spirit begins working with you. Remember, whatever measure you use, that's what's used to give back to you—and that's not just about giving things but about giving faith to God (Luke 6:38). That is going to have an effect on you, and you are going to have an effect on others. So many more than you think!

I believe that you are going to get to the place where you only do what the Father says and say what the Father says, just like Jesus. And that's called living blessed—walking in goodness, power, faith, mercy, and love. It's called moving from one God-given desire and goal to the next, and affecting others for good as you go.

The next thing you know, God will start honoring you in everything, and I do mean everything, that you do—little things, big things, and everything in between. Your faith becomes so instinctive that you use it all the time, and it paves the way before you even get to where you're going. You become a magnet for what's good, a light that can't be hidden for those who need it, and a blessing going somewhere to bless *all* the time, not just some of the time. I call that the blessing cycle.

Honor God in all that you do, but especially your faith in His Word, and watch how He honors you. Once that blessing cycle gets rolling, watch out! You are going to instinctively start asking and receiving "whatsoever" you ask in Jesus' name. You'll instinctively live with more integrity, discipline, and honor toward God and other people He puts in your life.

Your visions and dreams, even with all the conditions and responsibilities they require, will not look impossible to you, but doable! You'll instinctively adopt an even more fearless attitude when it comes to believing God for big things.

It's all faith anyway, so you might as well use it for what is on your heart and honor God as you go. After all, you are God's child, Jesus gave you permission to live with abundance, and "Your Everything Is His Anything!" As you reach out in faith and honor God, He is not only going to answer you and bless you, but He's going to *honor* you, too. The world is going to call you blessed!

CHAPTER ELEVEN

When Will We Believe What Jesus Says About What We Say?

*"For verily I say unto you, That whosoever shall **say** unto this mountain, Be thou removed, and be thou cast into the sea; and shall not doubt in his heart, but shall believe that those things which he **saith** shall come to pass; he **shall have whatsoever he saith**. Therefore **I say** unto you, What things soever ye desire, when ye pray, believe that ye receive them, and ye shall have them."*

Mark 11:23-24

What did *Jesus* say right there? The verse is His teaching, and He's telling us that we have power. Our power isn't only in our faith in God but in our *words*. Again, Jesus Christ is the One who gave us this teaching. And, again, this is just one more of His teachings that many who claim to love Him absolutely loathe.

Mark 11:23 is made fun of in churches today. Believers laugh about it and mock all who follow this teaching by calling it things like a "blab it and grab it" or a "name it and claim it" teaching. This is a mockery of Jesus Christ's words.

In books, articles, blogs, sermons, and comments strewn all over the web, people mock Jesus—and then go on to say how much they love Him.

In Jesus, we find the words of life—a life that is more abundant than life without Him. If He said that our words matter, then our words matter! Unlike a lot of Christians today, Jesus did not have a form of godliness but deny the power thereof (2 Timothy 3:5). He *was* God, in the flesh, and His words are full of life, even if our natural mind tilts just reading them.

Whoever discounts the power of words may be a wonderful preacher or teacher of other parts of the Word, but when it comes to the part about *human* words? They don't get it yet! So, just let their mockery roll off of you like water off a duck's back. Let it go—and go with what Jesus said instead. Once you start doing this, with faith and regularity, you will see the great power that resides in your own faith-filled words.

How Do You Move an Obstacle Out of View?

Jesus gave us a fundamental truth in Mark 11:23 about the power of our words. You could say this is the "how to" way to handle obstacles, and it's very simple. Don't be fooled into thinking it is too easy to work. It works if we work it! Read what Jesus said again: *"For verily I say unto you, That whosoever shall **say** unto this mountain, Be thou removed, and be thou cast into the sea; and shall not doubt in his heart, but shall believe* *that those things which he **saith** shall come to pass; he **shall have** whatsoever he saith."*

Speak with authority and faith. Visualize that mountainous obstacle in your life. Tell it where to go. Just like asking for "whatsoever" and believing you will get it because Jesus said it, have faith in the truth He also told you about the power of your words. You can literally *speak* obstacles right out of your own sight—this does not make sense in the natural, but it is a spiritual law that Jesus Christ revealed to us.

Unbelievers are now using this, but I don't care how many good affirmations you use, there is nothing like the Word of God coming out of your mouth. We Christians call it confessing the Word. When you insert yourself in the Word and make it personal and then confess it over your life, your life begins to change from the spiritual realm first. Your words are a force in your own life. Jesus was telling us in Mark 11:23 that we can *aim* our words at something and create movement—we are moving the obstacle, the problem, whatever it is, out of sight the moment we start telling it to go and declaring what we want.

Be direct. Take authority. Tell that obstacle to move from your sight! Think about the visual imagery that Jesus used in this verse. Mountains are huge, you can't see around them, and they loom in your sight like immovable masses that would take you days and maybe weeks to scale. Jesus says to *speak* to them.

Jesus didn't use the words *mountain* and *sea* without purpose. Where is the only place you can hide a mountain from view? In the sea. It's a perfect example. So, what are you looking at today? What is in your way? What is blocking your path? What can't you see around? What seems immovable, fixed, and unchangeable that you just don't want clouding up your view anymore?

"Be thou removed" is a command. It's Jesus telling you how to get rid of that obstacle in your life. Where is your obstacle going to go if you start speaking to it with authority and faith? It's going one place—*down!* That's right! Tell that thing where to go. Use the power God has given you. He formed the world with the words of His mouth. Now, you form your future with the words of your mouth. Use your words. You have the right to do this. You have the power and authority to do this. Jesus wouldn't have told you that you could if you couldn't!

Is Your "Mountain" Hearing Your Voice?

I don't complain about mountains, I speak to them— "Get out of my sight," I say, "Be thou removed!" It seems crazy to some people to talk to problems directly, but that's what works. You may think that words are only for people or God to hear, but your "mountain" also needs to hear your voice.

The "mountain" may be sickness, debt, hatred, or malice. Whatever it is that you don't want and that you think you're just "stuck with" can be unstuck with the words of your mouth. It's a spiritual law that you need to practically do. You need to see your words as dissolving the adhesive that has kept that obstacle or problem in place for so long.

If you want to get rid of something in your life (and you *do* need to get rid of some things in order to make room for the good things you want), just start talking to that problem. I know that it can be hard to focus on what's *good* when you're staring at a mountain of what's *not good*, but that is exactly where you must start. Faith starts with the mountain still in view. Faith doesn't begin when everything is great; it begins the day you decide to begin…and that could be when you're staring at an obstacle you want removed.

Problems bend to faith and words. Jesus told us the place that the problem should go, and that is down—but it's not just going to slink down. It's got to be *cast* down. In other words, when it comes to using faith, an obstacle must be moved with *force*. What force? The force of your *words*.

Don't fall into that natural-minded trap of making excuses for the obstacle being there. There may be a very good reason that obstacle exists, but it doesn't matter. The mountain must move when it is hit with the force of your faith-filled *words*.

Don't complicate your situation by trying to climb the obstacle—you aren't the one who needs to conquer the obstacle by getting all entangled with the problem. That means no overthinking it. That means no excuses for why some of the mountain might need to stay. No. *All* of the mountain needs to go down—all of it! Again, what's going to cast it out of view? Your faith-filled *words*.

God did not create you to be a mountain-climber. You have been given the truth by Jesus Christ so that you can be a mountain-mover. Move that thing into the "sea." Dissolve its very image from your view. See with the eyes of faith that it is moving every single time you open your mouth with faith and authority and give it its direction—out of your sight!

Are You Letting Religious People
Turn Your Problem into a Holy Relic?

If you let religious people tell you what they think about it, they'll have you canonize the problem and make it a holy relic in your life. Do you really want that? Do you want the obstacle to be "Christianized" or do you want it to go away?

Choose ye this day whom you will serve; choose whose words you are going to believe! Jesus has the insight. He revealed a spiritual answer that affects natural problems, and the sooner you listen to Him and start speaking from a place of faith and authority, the sooner that problem is going to start moving.

Some people will say, "But I'm trying, Brother Jesse," and all I can say back to you is that there is nowhere in the Bible that it tells you to be a "tryer" of the Word—but it does say that you should be a doer. I know that sounds harsh, but I wouldn't be doing you any favors if I told you it's OK to not do what Jesus said.

> We are the commanders in our own lives—what we say matters, and when we mix faith in it, what we say is what goes! Accept that truth.

When it comes to the teachings of Jesus Christ, you are dealing with revealed knowledge about the way God has made the world to work. The words of Jesus are true whether we believe them or not—and they are true whether we use them correctly or not.

I don't "try" to use my faith—I use my faith. I command my faith to do its job. Jesus gave you and me the power to *command*. We are the commanders in our own lives—what we say matters, and when we mix faith in it, what we say is what goes! Accept that truth. Just accept it. Don't dumb-down your power. Don't negate your power by thinking you don't have any—you have more power than you even need because you have the power of attorney to use the name of Jesus! So, you've got more than enough power.

Not only do you have the power to tell the devil where to go, you are commanded by Jesus to tell him and the obstacle he threw in your path to get under your feet—below sight level. Realize that its very presence is an affront to the life that Jesus came to give you. You were created for abundant life—a good life. If something is standing in the way of that, you do what you must in the natural, but remember that the spiritual force of your words is going to be the most powerful tool you've got in unearthing that problem.

Any obstacle in the way of your "life and that more abundantly" kind of life is *not* for you, and it has to go in Jesus' name! It's not holy. It's not good. It's not God's will for you to be stuck and trapped with a glaring, mountainous problem. Be forceful with your words and speak them in faith knowing that the Word is backing you up—Jesus is backing you up.

Are You Taking Matters into Your Own Mouth?

Speaking to the problem directly is a whole lot different than speaking about the problem to yourself and to others. Rehearsing how bad the problem is won't change the situation. Other people's sympathy won't get rid of the problem either. I know some people who'd rather cry about their mountain for 50 years than just obey Jesus and start taking their God-given authority and speaking to it. They have become so accustomed to the problem that they can't visualize their life without it.

You need to start "seeing" your life without the problem. See it in your spirit. Visualize it with your mind. When you pray, call those things that be not as though they already are, like Abraham did (Romans 4:17). Say that the mountain is moving out of sight. Say that it's on its descent into the sea. Say it's going down, in Jesus' mighty name!

I know that when you are going through something, the support of others is important and sometimes really a blessing. But be careful about how far you go with talking about your mountain. While it's nice to have people who understand what you're going through, you have to take matters into your own *mouth* if you want to get rid of that thing.

For some people, they've just got to get angry enough at the problem to start talking. If that's you, ask God to give you a better perspective of just how much that mountain is robbing you—start seeing it as a work of the devil that is stealing, killing, and destroying some aspect of your good life! You deserve everything Jesus came to give you. Anything outside of that doesn't have to remain in your life.

Always keep Satan "low" in your own mind—don't give his works any extra energy by talking about them all the time. You've got a destiny. You've got a destination to reach. The devil is a flesh devil, in that all he's really got to sway you with is your senses. But you've got God on the inside, and you have way more power than you think. Remember you are the head and not the tail, above and not beneath—keep your eyes on Jesus and on what He said, and don't magnify the mountain by bemoaning it too much. Yes, it's a pain, but it's going into the sea by the power of your words—end of statement.

God's Word will make you ride on the high places. It will lift your eyes to see from a higher and more spiritual perspective. It'll remind you of the authority you have in Christ Jesus. So, take matters into your own mouth and start moving that mountain. You've got enough faith, and the obstacle needs to know it.

Are You Ready for Obstacles to Get Out and Desires to Move In?

I want you to notice that right after Mark 11:23, Jesus says this—and notice that it is about *desires*: *"Therefore I say unto you, What things soever ye desire, when ye pray, believe that ye receive them, and ye shall have them."* So, He moves right from talking about moving *obstacles out* to talking about moving *desires in*.

"Believe that ye receive" is a single thing to do—it's not believing, and then receiving. It's believing you've received at the time that you prayed. This is another spiritual concept that shows us that all things begin somewhere else. It starts in the spirit. We move in the spirit. We speak, and the spirit-world shifts, which then begins a shifting in the natural world. Things are "coming to pass," in that they are moving either away from us or toward us, depending on our words and our beliefs.

The manifestation is when you see with your natural eyes the consequences of your words and your faith. But everything you see by that time was already yours in the spirit before it manifested in the natural. So, as you use your words, and continue to use your words, just know that you aren't "waiting for" anything to happen.

Obstacles are moving out. They began moving the moment you began speaking. Desires are moving in. They began moving toward you the moment you began believing you had them when you prayed.

So, asking for *"what things soever ye desire"* is Jesus telling you that it's OK to desire something. But if you want that desire, "when ye pray, believe that ye receive them" the moment you pray. Know that they are coming to you. "Ye shall have them!" Why? Because God loves you, that's the way faith works, and you are doing what He said.

Is There a Glitch in Moving Mountains and Receiving Desires?

Yes, there is a definite reason why some people cannot move mountains or receive desires—and it is a heart issue that gets in the way. Mark 11:25-26 says, *"And when ye stand praying, forgive, if ye have ought against any: that your Father also which is in Heaven may forgive you your trespasses. But if ye do not forgive, neither will your Father which is in Heaven forgive your trespasses."*

You really throw a wrench in the fire when you don't forgive people. It can totally stop you from being able to use your faith properly—it clouds your heart and your mind so you can't even function as well as you'd like spiritually. Consequently, you don't receive as well as you'd like. Mountains *stay* and desires *stay away* when there is unforgiveness.

It's not easy to forgive some people. They aren't just thorns in the flesh; they are complete bushes! But no matter what they did, that offense isn't worth hamstringing your future over. If you let them, they will not only have taken you for a ride with the original thing they did, but they'll keep you locked up spiritually and keep stealing from you.

The joy of forgiveness is in realizing that what they did doesn't have power over you anymore. With the sheer act of forgiving, you are freed. *You.* Seek the Lord about this and let Him reveal the roots, and then actively pull them up—because your own future is at stake. It's worth the effort to forgive so that all things are right between not just you and them, but between you and God.

Free yourself by letting them off the hook, even if what they did was so wrong nobody can believe it, and even if they seem to have gotten away with it. Remember that God sees everything. Put it in His hands. Forgive so that you can be forgiven—and so that you won't clog the pipes of faith, so to speak! You want to have a free-flowing heart that believes easily, and a mouth that has no problem speaking to the mountain with faith. *No* offense in the world is worth your future.

Have You Ever Prayed So Strongly That God Sent an Angel for Your Words?

I really believe with every fiber of my being that *everything* you need and desire is something that Christ enjoys giving and seeing come to pass. *"And whatsoever ye shall ask in My name, that will I do, that the Father may be glorified in the Son. If ye shall ask any thing in My name, I will do it"* (John 14:13-14).

There are many beings who serve God that you can't see, but who move upon command. I'm talking about angels of God. They aren't fat little babies with harps who sit around on clouds all day! They are powerful spiritual beings who serve God first, and will come for your words if they match the Lord's.

They move between dimensions and worlds. While these beings move according to God's will, they will also fight on behalf of men and women of faith who use God's Word. And they also help bring us the answers to our prayers if we have asked in Jesus' name, and if we're believing by faith and speaking in accordance with God's Word. How else do you think so many things in the spirit get done?

Angels bring God glory, and they do what He says. It's their joy to do His will. They'll also do what we say, if we are saying what *He* says! One day, when you cross over, you are going to be blown away at the spiritual army of beings who serve the Lord. Who knows? You may get to see some right here on earth while you are living, if it is God's will—but it's better if you don't see and have faith. It's actually the way God intended things to be.

This is our world. The Bible says that the heavens are the Lord's, but the earth He's given to the children of men (Psalm 115:16). *We* are those children! God wants us to enjoy the place He's created for us, to live by the Sspirit while we're walking in this physical flesh. We'll see angels forever when we pass. For now, they will mostly remain invisible to us.

Still, be careful how you treat strangers—you really never know who you are talking to, or who is there to give an account to God for your actions. God sometimes sends them for reasons we don't quite know. Hebrews 13:1-2 wouldn't be there if God didn't want you to have a heads-up: *"Let brotherly love continue. Be not forgetful to entertain strangers: for thereby some have entertained angels unawares."* Imagine that!

Angels are spoken of all over the Bible. One of my favorites is in Daniel 10:12, where an angel reveals to Daniel that it was his actual *words* that brought the visit: *"...for from the first day that thou didst set thine heart to understand, and to chasten thyself before thy God, thy words were heard, and I am come for thy words."* Another translation says, *"your words were heard, and I have come as a consequence of [and in response to] your words"* (AMPC).

The angel revealed right then to us that our words can, in fact, draw the presence of angels. Our words are containers that are continually being poured into the ears of those in the spirit realm. They hold our destiny because they have power—they don't just cause us and other people to react certain ways; they also go up to the Lord, and sometimes even angels come because of words.

So, when Jesus told us to ask anything in His name, He wasn't playing around—He was telling you that your words are powerful. The act of asking requires that you *speak*. What you say is going to be heard by the Lord. Angels will get in on the project to bring your words to pass as well, if the Lord wills it—and we know what His will is because we know His Word.

God's Word *is* His will. He doesn't break His Word, but as I said earlier, sometimes He will even go above and beyond it to make things happen. That day, Daniel's words drew God to send an angel on His behalf—one that showed himself to Daniel's natural eyes and deliberately told him that he'd come because of Daniel's words.

Now, we know that all scripture is in the Bible so that we'll understand God's ways. Like 2 Timothy 3:16 says, all the scriptural stories and instructions are given by inspiration of God, and they are *"profitable for doctrine, for reproof, for correction, for instruction in righteousness."* What do we learn from Daniel's angel in that short verse? We learn that *words* can draw the divine. The right words bring divine attention. What are your words bringing?

Are you working with God and yourself? Or are you working against God and yourself? When you pray, do you believe that you receive? When you pray, do you ask God for what is really on your heart—and do you ask in faith? Do fear and dread rule your heart more than faith in God?

Do you realize that this life we are living is seen by forces that we cannot see? Do you realize that your words matter—not only to you, but to them? When Jesus heard complaints about His disciples and how they didn't wash their hands before eating, He said it wasn't what went into a man that mattered, but what came out. In other words, food going into your mouth with dirty hands isn't nearly as important as the words coming out of your mouth on a daily basis.

We all mess up. We all say the wrong thing at one time or another. We all doubt or fall short of the glory of God. But we also *all* get an opportunity to get it right again! Every day is a new opportunity to have faith in God—another chance to sow the Word into our heart and to let it come sailing out of our mouth.

Your heart, your mind, and your mouth have the potential to draw divine favor and blessing into your life. Don't use your mouth for what you do not even want! Put God's Word deep in your heart, and then watch your thoughts and watch your lips. Remember that God loves you and He is listening, and He will "come for your words" if your words are worth coming for. You will have what you ask for, and you will have what you say.

So, ask whatsoever ye desire. Say what you desire. If two or more agree as touching anything in prayer, Matthew 18:19-20 says that God will be in their midst and bring it to pass—that's divine attention, and all you need is two to be in agreement. You are one and since the Word doesn't say that second even has to be another person, Jesus can be your "two." Remember, you and the Lord make a majority.

As this book is coming to a close, I want you to know that God has given you strengths and He means for you to use them in this life. He's given you desires and He means for you to have them. He's given you dreams and He means for you to see them come to pass. He's got to be involved for all of that to happen, so keep Him close in your heart. Don't let go.

Use what you've been given knowing that your faith is from God, your soul is precious in His sight, and your words are powerful tools He's given you to use—so use them well! Use His Word and create the life you want. Use your mouth and ask Him in faith for "whatsoever" you desire.

There is nothing you can't have and nothing you can't do with God. *"With men this is impossible; but with God **all** things are possible"* (Matthew 19:26). Everything good that you could ever desire or need is available in Christ's command to "ask anything in My name"—so *ask*. Your *everything* really is His *anything!*

God bless you as you take what you've learned and *go!* Go with joy, go with faith, and go out into this world with love and not fear, knowing that God is with you and great things lie ahead for you. It's time for you to have what God said you could have and do what God said you could do. So go and do something great! Go and get the life that God has for you. May God's light be your guide, and may all the desires of your heart come to pass!

Prayer of Salvation

"For God so loved the world, that He gave His only begotten Son, that whosoever believeth in Him should not perish, but have everlasting life. For God sent not His Son into the world to condemn the world; but that the world through Him might be saved."

John 3:16-17

God loves the world. He sent His Son, Jesus, to make a way for all of us to be free—from guilt, from shame, and from every sin and misstep, no matter how big or small. Salvation removes the heavy chains of sin and a life lived apart from our Maker. Christ's death and resurrection on the cross was sacrificial. He did it for you, for me, and for the whole world so that we could have that blank slate and simply start again.

Accepting God's plan of salvation through Jesus Christ is the first step because, as Mark 8:36 says, *"For what shall it profit a man, if he shall gain the whole world, and lose his own soul?"* It doesn't matter how many goals you achieve or dreams you fulfill, if you don't have Jesus, you are missing out. Nothing is as important as being right with God in your heart—and by accepting Christ, you are doing just that.

If you don't know my Jesus today, if you've never prayed a prayer of salvation, or if you just need to come back home to God where you belong, would you take a moment and pray with me today? This prayer below is a guide. Feel free to talk from your heart. Wherever you are right now, no matter what your situation, God will meet you where you are—He will hear your prayer, loose the chains of bondage off of your soul, and set you free with the blood of His precious Son, Jesus. Open your heart and pray this with me now:

"God, thank You for loving me enough to send Your Son. I know that I need You. I believe that You are my God, my Maker, and my Father—and I believe that You sent Your only begotten Son to die for me. I believe that He died and rose again for me, too, so that I could be washed clean of all my sins. Jesus, come into my life right now. Wash me clean and create a new heart in me now. Thank You for paying the price for me. From this point on, I will seek to serve You and love You, and I ask You to help me to find my destiny in You—to be whole in every area of my life. May Your blessings follow me all the days of my life as I learn from You. Thank You, Jesus, for saving me! My new life starts right now, Lord. This is my God-day and I'm never turning back! I want the best You have for me, in every way."

If you have prayed this prayer or if this book has helped you to create a good life in Christ, would you write and let me know? Please write to me at:

Jesse Duplantis Ministries
PO Box 1089
Destrehan, LA 70047-1089
www.jdm.org

I encourage you to begin reading your Bible for wisdom and listening to positive messages that will encourage your faith. Find a church in your area where you can attend, meet others, and grow in your faith. God has so much in store for you as you follow Him. New people. New ideas about how to live well. New insights for your own destiny with God. Your *everything* really is His *anything*, and I believe that His best for your life is just beginning. God bless you as you go and grow! And if I don't get to see you here on earth, I'll meet you in Heaven. Who knows? I may live next door to you—I'll be at your house every day! Ha! Remember that as you grow, God always loves you, He's always with you, and no matter what, you always have victory in Him!

—Jesse Duplantis

About the Author

Jesse Duplantis, a best-selling author, has sold more than 1.2 million copies of his books worldwide, with many being translated into multiple languages, as well as Braille editions for the blind. He is the founder of Jesse Duplantis Ministries, located in the Greater New Orleans area of south Louisiana.

In full-time ministry since 1978, with over four decades of evangelistic ministry behind him, Jesse has become known and loved worldwide for his strong, down-to-earth messages, his belief that nothing is impossible with God, and his humorous take on experiences in the believer's life. Generations of believers have been inspired by his messages, and countless numbers have come to know Jesus Christ as Savior through his ministry.

Known for his unflinching, status-quo-breaking messages and his long-standing integrity in ministry, Jesse continues to draw large audiences of believers through television, social media, and meetings held around the world. With a television ministry that spans the globe, Jesse Duplantis continues to be one of the most sought-after Christian speakers today. With speaking engagements booked years in advance, Jesse Duplantis continues to keep an intense traveling schedule, flying throughout the United States and the world preaching the Gospel of Jesus Christ.

With no booking agents pursuing meetings for him and no set fees imposed upon churches for speaking engagements, Jesse Duplantis chooses his outreach meetings based on the same two criteria he always has: invitations that come in, and prayer over each one. This uncommon way of scheduling means his many followers may find him speaking in some of the largest churches and venues in America and the world, as well as a great many small and growing congregations, too. No church is too big or small for the Holy Spirit, as he says.

Side by side with his wife Cathy, the co-founder and chief of staff of Jesse Duplantis Ministries and the senior pastor of JDM Covenant Church in Destrehan, Louisiana, Jesse continues to fulfill his life's calling by daily taking up the Great Commission of Jesus Christ: *"Go ye into all the world, and preach the Gospel to every creature"* (Mark 16:15).

Through television broadcasts, books, and other ministry products, as well as through evangelistic meetings, the JDM website, the JDM app, social media, and *Voice of the Covenant* magazine, Jesse Duplantis continues to expand his reach while maintaining his roots. Jesus is the center of his life. The salvation of lost people and the growth of believers is the purpose of his ministry. And for both he and his wife, every day is another day to *"Reach People and Change Lives, One Soul at a Time"* with the Gospel of Jesus Christ and the success-producing principles of the Word of God.

Other Books by Jesse Duplantis

Advance in Life
From Revelation to Inspiration to Manifestation

The Big 12
*My Personal Confidence-Building Principles
for Achieving Total Success*

Living at the Top
How to Prosper God's Way and Avoid the Pitfalls of Success

For by IT…FAITH
If You Don't Know What "IT" is, You Won't Have It!

DISTORTION
The Vanity of Genetically Altered Christianity

The Everyday Visionary
Focus Your Thoughts, Change Your Life

What in Hell Do You Want?

Wanting a God You Can Talk To

Jambalaya for the Soul
Humorous Stories and Cajun Recipes from the Bayou

Breaking the Power of Natural Law
Finding Freedom in the Presence of God

God is Not Enough, He's Too Much!
How God's Abundant Nature Can Revolutionize Your Life

Heaven: Close Encounters of the God Kind

The Ministry of Cheerfulness

Other Content:

Other ministry resources by Jesse Duplantis are available through www.jdm.org, the JDM App, and TotalJDM.org (a subscription service of Jesse Duplantis Ministries).

To contact Jesse Duplantis Ministries
with prayer requests, praise reports, or comments,
or to schedule Jesse Duplantis at your church, conference, or seminar,
please write, call, or email:

JESSE DUPLANTIS MINISTRIES

PO Box 1089
Destrehan, LA 70047
985-764-2000
www.jdm.org

We also invite you to connect with us on social media:

- Facebook: /JesseDuplantisMinistries
- Twitter: @jesse_duplantis
- Instagram: @jesseduplantisministries
- YouTube: /jesseduplantismin
- Pinterest: /JesseDuplantisMinistries

The Harrison House Vision

Proclaiming the truth and the power
of the Gospel of Jesus Christ with excellence.
Challenging Christians
to live victoriously,
grow spiritually,
know God intimately.

Connect with us on

f Facebook @ HarrisonHousePublishers

and 📷 Instagram @ HarrisonHousePublishing

so you can stay up to date with news

about our books and our authors.

Visit us at **www.harrisonhouse.com**

for a complete product listing as well as

monthly specials for wholesale distribution.